GETTING A FIX ON VOCABULARY

USING WORDS IN THE NEWS

THE SYSTEM OF AFFIXATION AND COMPOUNDING IN ENGLISH

RAYMOND C. CLARK & JANIE L. DUNCAN

NEWS PHOTOGRAPHS BY MICHAEL JERALD

PRO LINGUA ⬤ ASSOCIATES

Published by **Pro Lingua Associates**
P.O. Box 1348, Brattleboro, Vermont 05302
Orders: 800-366-4775
Phone: 802-257-7779
Email: Orders@ProLinguaAssociates.com
Webstore: www.ProLinguaAssociates.com
SAN 216-0579

*At Pro Lingua,
our objective is to foster
an approach to learning and teaching which
we call **Interplay**, the **inter**action of language
learners and teachers with their materials,
with the language and the culture, and
with each other in active, creative,
and productive **play**.*

Copyright © 1990 by Raymond C. Clark and Janie L. Duncan

ISBN 0-86647-038-7

The publisher wishes to thank the Michael Jerald Photo News Service Ink (MJPNSI) and his ubiquitous friend and accomplice, Edgar Sather.

This book was set in Clearface, Bodoni, and Century type by Stevens Graphics of Brattleboro, Vermont, and printed and bound by Sheridan Books, MI.

Designed by Arthur A. Burrows.

Printed in the United States of America.
6th printing 2005. 15,500 copies in print.

Contents

Foreword
to the Teacher

Why use this book?

This text is designed for high-intermediate/advanced-level students of English as a second language and high school-level native English speakers.

The primary purpose of this book is to increase the students' *awareness* of affixation and compounding in English, and to help them develop their *skill* in word analysis. This awareness and skill can help turn unknown words into words that are, if not fully understood, at least partially understood. By recognizing the functions of words (noun, verb, adjective, adverb), the students can more easily grasp the meaning of whole sentences.

Secondly, an increased awareness of affixes and bases can facilitate vocabulary expansion by helping students see connections among various forms, e.g., contain, maintain, retain, unretained, detainable, detention. In this way, learning one word can lead to learning a bundle of words.

This text will also help develop spelling and pronunciation skills by identifying patterns that occur when bases and affixes are combined, e.g., explode, explosion.

A fourth purpose is to increase the students' vocabulary. To this end, we have provided fictitious, "generic" new stories at the end of each lesson. Although the primary purpose of these stories is to showcase selected compounds, affixes, and bases, the students can be encouraged to develop their knowledge of words and phrases that are commonly used in the media.

How to use the book:

This book has been designed to facilitate self-directed learning. However, it would still be useful for the teacher to check that students are progressing satisfactorily, and to see if they have questions. Hence, a regular procedure, at its simplest, would be:

1. *Assign* the lesson for homework.

2. *Follow up* to see what questions the students have from the assignment.

Follow up can also be more detailed:

1. Have the students brainstorm (fill up the blackboard or poster paper) words exhibiting affixes that are the focus of the lesson.

2. Have the students close their books while you read aloud the news story. Ask the students to tap their pencils on their desks every time you say a word that contains the featured affixes. Alternatively, have them write it down.

3. Read the news story sentence-by-sentence (or paragraph-by-paragraph). After each sentence, ask a few questions: Who? What? When? Where? Why? How long? etc. Vary this approach by having students read while you listen for pronunciation.

4. Give a quiz based on the featured affixes or the news story.

5. Copy the news story and then white out all the featured affixes or words. Then re-copy the story and have the students fill in the blanks.

6. Copy and bring in a real news story and have the students go on an affix hunt, circling the featured affixes or all the affixes that have been studied.

The text can also be used mostly as an in-class activity. In this situation, a typical pattern of work might be:

1. Introduce the featured affixes.

2. Go through the explanations, adding elaborations of your own.

3. Have the students work individually or in pairs on the exercises, without looking at the answer key.

4. Go over the students' answers, clarifying and explaining where necessary.

5. Read through the news story, or assign it for homework.

Acknowledgements

We would like to thank the many students at the Center for International Banking Studies in Istanbul, who used the preliminary editions of this book. Their comments and questions were very helpful.

We would also like to thank our colleague Melinda Taplin for her comments and Nazlı Kıral for typing the manuscript.

Raymond C. Clark
Janie L. Duncan
June, 1989

INTRODUCTION

There are thousands of words in English. Learning these words is a big problem for students of English. However, there are ways to solve this problem. One way is to become familiar with the process of word formation in English. Take for example, the phrase:

Underground Explosions

The word **underground** is really two separate words, **under** and **ground**. This illustrates a process of word formation that is called *compounding*. Many English words are formed this way.

The word **explosions** is formed by a process called *affixation*. A base carries the main meaning of the word, and affixes add to the meaning. The base here is **plod**, which comes from Latin and means "making a noise by clapping the hands together" or "noise."

In the word **explosions** there are three different affixes. **Ex-** is attached in front of the base and is called a *prefix*. **-sion** is attached after the base and is called a *suffix*. Another suffix, **-s**, indicates the word is plural, and it is attached to the singular form of the word **explosion**.

Therefore, an analysis of the word shows us this:

ex-	plo(d)	-sion	-s
out of, from	noise	the act of (also shows the word is a noun)	plural

As you can see from the example, the process of analyzing a word into its parts will not always give an exact meaning for the word. Words often change their meanings, especially after they are borrowed from one language and put to use in another language. But analysis will help. It is especially important and useful to learn the affixes because there are not many of them and they are very commonly used in English. A chart of the affixes that we will study in this book appears on page 3.

You can also see that it is helpful, if not necessary, to know the meaning of the base in order to fully understand the word. But the list of bases is very long and we would not expect you to learn or know them all. In this book we will work only with some of the more common bases. There is a glossary of common bases in the appendix of this book.

You will also see in the example that there are some spelling and pronunciation changes when affixes are added to bases.

Word analysis is not an exact, precise process which will always give you the complete meaning. But developing some skill in taking words apart will help you better understand what you read, and it will help you increase your vocabulary.

Throughout the text, we have used readings and vocabulary that you will frequently see in the news. The news stories are fictitious—that is, they are not real—but they are similar to news stories that appear regularly in newspapers. So this book will also introduce you to words that you will see again and again in any newspaper. When you have finished this book you can continue your vocabulary development with the help of the daily newspaper.

In the back of this book there is an answer key so you can check your answers to the exercises.

Affix Chart

Lesson Number	Prefixes		Function/ Meaning	Lesson Number	Suffixes		Function/ Meaning
5	un- in-	non-	Negative	3	-er		"Doer" Noun
				4	-ist -ian	-ant -ary	
6	anti- a- dis-	mal- mis-		8	-en -ify	-ate -ize	Verb
7	uni- mono- bi- tri- pan-	multi- semi- poly- equi-	Quantity	9	-ance -ity -hood	-ship -ness	Noun
				10	-ion -ment -ism	-age -dom	
8	en-	be-	Verb				
15	pre- post- inter-	intra- extra-	Position	11	-able -less	-al -en	Adjective
16	super- sur- epi- hyper-	sub- hypo- para-	Relationship	12	-ful -y	-ous -ary	
				13	-ish -ic	-ive	
17	ex- in- ad-	ab- trans- pro-	Movement	14	-ly -ward	-wise	Adverb
18	de- re-	se-					
19	syn- co-	contra-	With or Against				

Lesson 1

Inflections

In the word **explosion** we saw that the final affix **-s** made the word plural. This kind of affix is called an inflection, and it is somewhat different from ex- and -sion. It is really a grammatical affix and is used throughout the language. In other words, almost every noun in English can be made plural by simply adding **-s**. We say "almost" because, as you know, there are irregular noun plurals such as **man/men**. Also, there are some spelling changes in English when inflections are affixed, so that the plural of **dish** is **dishes,** and the plural of **dictionary** is **dictionaries**. But these are matters that are covered in grammar and spelling. We will not cover them in detail in this book.

In this lesson we will simply remind you of the eight inflectional suffixes in English. They are:

Inflectional Suffix	Example	Grammatical Function
-ed	exploded	past tense or past participle
-en	hidden	past participle
-ing	planning	progressive form or present participle
-s	continues	third person singular verb
-s	explosions	plural
-'s	prosecutor's	possessive marker
-er	larger	comparative
-est	largest	superlative

Exercises

A. Read the following article once. Do it rapidly for general comprehension.

B. Go through the story again, and underline, circle, or highlight all the inflectional suffixes. Check your answers with the answer key.

C. Look in the glossary of bases at the back of the book for the meaning of in*vestig*ation, su*spect* and de*tain*. Whenever you see new words, look for their bases and check their meanings in the glossary.

Terrorist Conspiracy Uncovered

A spokesperson said today that federal police have detained 15 suspected terrorists. The police also discovered explosives hidden in a Westside warehouse, and several automatic weapons were taken from the apartment of one of the suspected terrorists.

The police raided four separate locations Thursday and apparently prevented a terrorist attack, a spokesperson for the prosecutor's office said in a telephone interview.

The detainees were under investigation for criminal conspiracy. According to security sources, they have been planning an attack to be carried out in an unnamed neighboring country.

Intelligence officers discovered the conspiracy, and warrants have been issued for the arrest of three ringleaders, the intelligence agency said.

Federal undercover agents, who normally head antiterrorism investigations, were handling the case.

Although this was not the agency's largest roundup of suspected terrorists, it is expected that the list of arrests may grow longer as the investigation continues.

TERRORIST HIDEOUT on West 164th St. raided by Feds Thursday.   MJP

Words with inflectional suffixes -ed, -en, -ing, -s, -'s, -er, -est:

Lesson 2

Compounds

Underground is a compound word. It is two words that are joined together to form a new word. Each part of the compound has a meaning. Usually it is fairly easy to understand the meaning of the compound word. But sometimes it helps to look at the *context* in which the word appears. This means you should look at the words that precede and follow the word you are analyzing.

Exercises

A.   The word **underground** is fairly easy to understand. It is **under** and **ground**, meaning beneath the surface of the earth. Can you guess the meaning of these?

      spokesperson

      ringleader

      undercover

      roundup

      warehouse

If you have any difficulty go back to the reading in Lesson 1 and look at the context. Then guess the meaning. Finally, check your guesses with the help of a dictionary.

1.   spokesperson   Guess _____

                            _____

                            Dictionary _____

                            _____

2.   ringleader   Guess _____

                              _____

                            Dictionary _____

                            _____

3.   undercover   Guess _____

                              _____

                            Dictionary _____

                            _____

4.   roundup   Guess _____

                              _____

                            Dictionary _____

                            _____

5.   warehouse   Guess _____

_____

Dictionary _____

_____

Looking at the context is a useful thing to do. If you cannot easily analyze a new word, be sure to study the context.

B.   Sometimes compound words are hyphenated. This means there is a line, called a hyphen, between the two parts of the word. Here are some examples. Give the meaning of the hyphenated compound. Try to do this by studying the context of the compound.

1. According to the Medical Association, the new technique could lower risks for heart-attack victims.

   heart-attack _____

2. The attack is likely to increase support for the right-wing political party.

   right-wing _____

3. The head of the seven-member committee has resigned.

   seven-member _____

4. The negotiator has arranged for a cease-fire between the warring countries.

   cease-fire _____

5. Investigators have concluded a five-year investigation of terrorism.

   five-year _____

6. The two nations have agreed to hold high-level talks.

   high-level _____

7. Government-backed soldiers have counterattacked.

   government-backed _____

8. You do not pay a tax on things which are purchased in a duty-free shop.

   duty-free _____

9. The new airline will offer a daily round-trip, smoke-free flight between the two eastern cities.

   round-trip _____

   smoke-free _____

10. The Boeing 737 is a twin-engine aircraft.

   twin-engine _____

C.   You may notice, as you read the news, that numbers are often used as part of a compound, for example, a three-day visit. In the space below write some compound phrases, similar to the example. Be careful that you don't make the second word of the hyphenated compound plural. For example, *a three-day visit* not *a three-days visit.*

_____   _____

_____   _____

_____   _____

_____   _____

D. Compounds are normally pronounced with the heaviest stress on the first part of the word. Practice saying these common compounds with stress on the first part of the word.

airline	thunderstorm	rainstorm
turbojet	daybreak	lifejackets
takeoff	planeload	mainland
jetliner	seaside	frogmen

E. The following story contains several compound words. First read the story for general comprehension; then read it for details and finally list all the compounds.

Airliner, Military Aircraft Collide

The national radio, NRT, announced today that an outbound turbojet aircraft, operated by the state-owned airline NATIONAIR collided with a military fighter-bomber. The collision occurred shortly after Flight 43's takeoff from Gulfside Airport. Flight 43 is a regularly scheduled, hour-long flight to Pelagia.

There were no eyewitnesses to the midair collision. It was first believed that the twin-engine jetliner had been struck by lightning. A heavy thunderstorm hit the area shortly before daybreak.

It is assumed that both aircraft went down in the Pacific Gulf. An airline spokeswoman has confirmed that the airliner was carrying a planeload of tourists going to the popular seaside resort of Pelagia.

Air-sea rescue teams dispatched to the area began the search for survivors in a heavy rainstorm. So far, none have been seen in the shark-infested waters, although several lifejackets were seen floating fifteen air-miles from the mainland coast. Navy frogmen will begin an underwater search for the wreckage when weather conditions permit.

CRASH SITE in shark-infested waters.   *Jerald Photos*

Compounds:

Lesson 3

The -er Suffix

One of the most common suffixes in English is -er, also spelled -or and -ar. It usually means "a person who (does something)."

teacher—a person who teaches
banker—a person who works in a bank
driver—a person who drives (a car)
player—a person who plays (a game)
collector—a person who collects (something)
beggar—a person who begs

It is not always easy to know which spelling to use, and there are other spelling problems, too. Look at **driver**, for example. The base is **drive**. When er is added, one of the e's is dropped. And with, **beg** the final consonant is doubled: **beggar**.

●*Note: Be careful that you don't confuse this -er suffix with the -er suffix that indicates comparison:* big—bigger.

A few -er words do not refer to people. They refer to a machine or thing that does something.

computer—a machine that computes
tractor—a vehicle that pulls things

There is an -ee suffix which shows that the person is the receiver of the action, not the doer of the action. In many cases there is a corresponding -er suffix.

employer—the owner of a business who employs workers
employee—the workers who are employed by the owner of the business

And there are a very few -er suffixes that are spelled -eer.

mountaineer—one who climbs mountains

Exercises

A. Rewrite these common words with the er/or/ar suffix. Then check your spelling with the answers in the back of the book.

report	_____	march	_____
credit	_____	kidnap	_____
write	_____	direct	_____
profess	_____	design	_____
buy	_____	trade	_____
lead	_____	vote	_____
manage	_____	riot	_____
employ	_____	law	_____
prosecute	_____	foreign	_____
work	_____	survive	_____
fly	_____	deal	_____
prison	_____	photograph	_____
plan	_____	demonstrate	_____
command	_____	advise	_____
inspect	_____	support	_____
export	_____	govern	_____
farm	_____	murder*	_____
hijack	_____	forecast	_____
lie	_____	act	_____
travel	_____	interpret	_____
investigate	_____	office	_____
labor*	_____	defect	_____
negotiate	_____		

*Note: A few English words end with -er/or/ar, but these endings are not suffixes. They are part of the word. For example: labor, murder, number, border, corner. Add some yourself: _____,

_____, _____, _____, _____.

B.   A few -er/or words are attached to bases that are not words.
     Use the list below to fill in the blanks.

soldier	minister	traitor
member	doctor	passenger
ambassador	chancellor	mayor
neighbor	victor	

   1. A person who travels in a car or plane is a _____ .

   2. A person who cares for sick people is a _____ .

   3. A person who belongs to an organization is a _____ .

   4. A person who is in the army is a _____ .

   5. A person who is in charge of an embassy is an _____ .

   6. A person who is the political leader of a city is a _____ .

   7. A person who defects to another country can be called a _____ .

   8. The leader of some countries is called a _____ .

   9. The person who is in charge of a ministry is a _____ .

  10. A person who lives near you is a _____ .

  11. A person who wins and gets the victory is a _____ .

C.   In some cases the suffix -er indicates "a machine or thing that . . ." Match these **er** things with their
     correct definitions.

   1. _____ bomber   a. a ship that carries airplanes
   2. _____ fighter   b. a device that cooks food
   3. _____ jetliner   c. a plane that attacks other planes
   4. _____ tanker   d. an electronic device that does computation
   5. _____ computer   e. an aircraft that does not have wings
   6. _____ aircraft carrier   f. a device that sends radio or TV signals
   7. _____ typewriter   g. a plane that carries passengers
   8. _____ transmitter   h. a ship that carries oil
   9. _____ recorder   i. a plane that attacks targets on the ground
  10. _____ helicopter   j. an instrument that records sound
  11. _____ cooker*   k. a machine that types letters

Note that a person who cooks is a cook.

D. The -ee suffix shows us the person is the receiver of a corresponding -er suffix. Complete these sentences:

1. The _____ is employed by the _____ .

2. The _____ was detained by the police.

3. The _____ trains the _____ .

4. The _____ pays the _____ .

5. The letter is addressed to the _____ .

Another variation of the -er suffix is the -eer suffix. There are not many of this type. Here are some:

6. A person who makes a profit is a _____ .

7. A person who writes pamphlets is a _____ .

8. A person is involved in an illegal racket is a _____ .

9. A person who sells things at an auction is an _____ .

10. A person who works voluntarily, that is without pay, is a _____ .

11. A person who works with engines is an _____ .

E. Read the following article once for general comprehension. Then read it for details, and list the words with -er/-or/-ar suffixes.

Negotiator Meets With Kidnappers

A government negotiator who has been meeting with kidnappers of the Antarctican Ambassador to Atlantis, met with reporters yesterday and released a statement from the Ambassador's captors. The kidnappers, identified as members of the little-known AMSAT faction, have demanded the release of all political prisoners in exchange for the Ambassador. The Ambassador was abducted two weeks ago, along with his political adviser and interpreter. The leader of the AMSAT group has also issued a warning to all foreigners now in Atlantis that unless AMSAT's demands are met, foreign workers and travelers will be in danger. Meanwhile, in

ANTARCTICAN AMBASSADOR

downtown Atlantia, the mayor and his councilors met with demonstrators who marched on City Hall. The marchers, reportedly supporters of AMSAT, have urged that the military prison commander be dismissed on grounds that political detainees have been tortured. The mayor assured the marchers that a special investigator would be appointed to look into the matter.

Words with -er suffixes:

Lesson 4

Other "Doer" Suffixes: -ist, -ian, -ant/-ent
and "Place" Suffixes: -ary/-ery/-ory/-ry

In addition to -er and its variants, there are three other suffixes that also mean "doer" of the activity: -ist, -ian, and -ant. There are some pronunciation or spelling changes when these suffixes are attached to a base.

> type — typist
> diet — dietician
> study — student

Notice that the -ian suffix is often spelled -cian. For example, a hairdresser who also helps women with their hands and faces to make them beautiful is called a **beautician**; some one who does magic is a **magician**. Also, many nationality names use this suffix or -an: **Canadian, Italian, Ethiopian, Mexican, Tibetan, Moroccan.**

● *Note: Not all words ending in* -ant/-ent, *are "doer" words.* Vacant *and* Permanent *are adjectives.*

-ary,-ery, -ory, and -ry are suffixes that often mean "a place where . . ." For example, a **winery** is a place where wine is made and a **granary** is a place where grain is stored.

However, there are many irregularities with this suffix, and the exact meaning of the word may not refer to a place. For example, it may refer to a person who does something, a type of material, or the study or practice of some subject.

> **Secretary** is a person, not a place for secrets
> **Stationery** means writing paper
> **Forestry** is the management of forests
> **Chemistry** is the study of chemicals

● *Note:* -ary *may also be an adjective suffix. It means "engaged in or connected with." We will study this suffix in lesson 12. For example:* **temporary, primary, stationary.**

Exercises

A. In the following sentences, give the appropriate -ist word.

1. A person who is involved in science is a _____ .

2. People who work in the fields of sociology, psychology and psychiatry are _____ , _____ , and _____ .

3. A person who is involved in economics is an _____ .
    a. Capitalism is practiced by _____ .
    b. Socialism is practiced by _____ .
    c. Communism is practiced by _____ .

4. Some writers:
    a. A person who writes dramas is a _____ .
    b. A person who writes novels is a _____ .
    c. A person who writes columns in a newspaper is a _____ (also called a journalist).

5. Some musicians:
    A _____ plays the guitar.
    A _____ plays the violin.
    A _____ plays the piano.
    A _____ plays cello.
    A _____ plays the flute.

6. Politicians who are realistic are _____ , and if they are idealistic, they are _____ .

7. A person who is very active, especially in political matters is an _____ . And if the person wants to have no government (anarchy), he/she is an _____ . An activist in environmental matters is an _____ . Ecology is the science of environmental balance. A person who studies it is an _____ .

8. Three criminals:
    One who burns buildings (the crime of arson): _____ .
    One who practices terror: _____ .
    One who rapes: _____ .

9. A person who tours a foreign country is a _____ .
    A person who drives a motor car is a _____ .

B. Match these -ian words with the appropriate description.

1. __ politician   a. Albert Einstein
2. __ musician   b. one who works in government
3. __ mathematician (and physicist)   c. a doctor
4. __ technician   d. the opposite of military
5. __ physician   e. a guitarist
6. __ civilian   f. one who operates technical instruments

C. Complete the following with an -ant/ent word. Use the list of bases below.

occup-   pati-   dissid-   immigr-   resid-
account-   migr-   consult-   oppon-

1. a worker who migrates from place to place: a _____ worker.

2. a person who is in the opposition: an _____ .

3. a person who charges money for giving advice: a _____ .

4. a person who gives financial advice: an _____ .

5. a person who occupies a place: an _____ .

6. a person who is sick: a _____ .

7. a person who immigrates into a country: an _____ .

8. a person who disagrees with the government: a _____ .

9. a person who lives in a place: a _____ .

D. Fill in the blanks with one of these words.

library   territory   bakery   directory
laboratory   factory   mortuary   diary
treasury   armory   chemistry   dictionary

1. Another word for "weapons" is "arms." Weapons would be kept in an _____ .

2. Bread is baked in a _____ .

3. Words are found in a _____ .

4. Telephone numbers are found in a _____

5. Daily notes are kept in a _____ .

6. A scientist works in a _____ .

7. Books are kept in a _____ .

8. The _____ department is concerned with money.

9. Goods are produced in a _____ .

10. Siberia is a huge _____ in Northern USSR.

11. Dead people are kept in a _____ before they are buried.

12. The study of matter is _____ .

E. Many nationalities are spelled with an -ian or -an suffix. Can you name a few?

_____   _____   _____

_____   _____   _____

_____   _____   _____

F. Read the following selection first for general comprehension; then for details. List all the words with suffixes that mean "one who" or "place where."

Awards for Artists and Scientists

PROF. BROWN-ARCHER

The Academy of Arts and Sciences today announced this year's winners in the fields of science, literature, ecology, music and economics. The winners will each receive cash prizes of $50,000, according to awards panelist Sir Arthur Lloyd.

Physicist Nils Groenig, notified of his award while working in his laboratory, celebrated with his research assistants, by toasting them with a bottle of champagne. Professor Anna Brown-Archer, a botanist at the University of Jackson, received the award for her work in plant genetics. The third scientist cited by the Academy was Dr. Rolf Steinmetz, a chemist at the University of Overberg.

The novelist and dramatist Pedro Garcia, an Antillian, was named the recipient of the literature prize. His latest novel, "The Diary of an Idealist" was acclaimed by the awards committee as a major contribution to world literature. The author, an outspoken dissident, is now a resident of Mexteca.

In the field of music, the award went to composer and pianist Gregor Kosnowski. Long considered one of the world's outstanding musicians, Kosnowski is best known for his piano concertos. A proponent of neo-romanticism, he is the resident conductor of the Thyme Conservatory of Music.

This year marked the first year that a prize was given to an environmentalist. Robert Rackham, a well-known forestry consultant and environmental activist, was praised for his work on the effects of deforestation in tropical rain forests.

The prize for economics was won by Martin Greenberg, whose recent book " The Proletarian and the Capitalist" is rapidly becoming a classic in its field.

"One who" and "place where" words:

Lesson 5

Negative Prefixes: un-, in-, non-

The word "prefix" has the prefix **pre-**, which means "before". Prefixes come at the beginning of a word. In this lesson and the one that follows, we will look at a group of prefixes that have a negative meaning.

One of the most common negative prefixes is **un-**, which means "not."

> **unimportant** — not important

Similar to **un-** is **in-**. This prefix, however, has different spellings. Sometimes it is spelled **im-**, **il-**, or **ir-**.

> in + active = inactive
> in + perfect = imperfect (in- becomes im- before b, m, and p)
> in + legal = illegal (in- becomes il before l)
> in + regular = irregular (in- becomes ir- before r)

● *Note: There is a prefix* in- *which means "in"or "into," as in* **inhabitant** *or* **immigrant**.

Another common negative prefix is **non-**, which also means "not."

> **nonresident** — not a resident

If the base begins with a capital letter, the prefix **non-** is usually attached to the base with a hyphen.

> non-Turkish

Exercises

A. You already know many words that begin with the prefix un-. List some below and compare them with a friend or a teacher, or check them in the dictionary.

_____	_____	_____
_____	_____	_____
_____	_____	_____
_____	_____	_____
_____	_____	_____

B. In the list below, add the prefix in- and its variants im-, ir-, il-, to the base form.

_____ dependent	_____ perfect	_____ balance	_____ sane
_____ mature	_____ moral	_____ secure	_____ literate
_____ responsible	_____ capable	_____ logical	_____ proper
_____ definite	_____ direct	_____ rational	

C. Complete these sentences with a word that is prefixed with non-.

1. She doesn't smoke. She's a _____ .
2. They are not Moslems. They are _____ .
3. Those countries are not aligned with the superpowers. They are _____ nations.
4. This flight does not stop between New York and London. It is _____ .
5. Gandhi was against violence. He practiced _____ .
6. This doesn't make sense. It's _____ .
7. These chemicals are not toxic. They are _____ .
8. He never conformed. He was a _____ .
9. He didn't pay his debts. He was guilty of _____ .
10. This population is not an Arab population. It is _____ .
11. You aren't a member of the club. You're a _____ .
12. The World Bank has a lot of loans that are not performing. They are _____ loans.

D. In the following story there are several negative prefixes, and a few in- prefixes that mean "in" or "into." List the words with negative prefixes only.

Nonresident Policy Questioned

The leader of the Lowland Independent Party (LIP), C. M. Unsap, yesterday called for the government to take action on the "nonresident" problem.

Citing statistics released by the Lowland Immigration Department, the opposition leader pointed out that in the past 5 years over 7,000 Highlanders have been granted refugee status in Lowland, and an estimated 20,000 others have entered the country illegally.

So far, the Lowland government has been uninterested in stopping the flow because illegal entrants have been willing to take jobs that most Lowlanders find unattractive and financially unrewarding, according to Unsap.

Mr. Unsap also pointed out that the Department of Labor has released statistics showing that unemployment among Lowlanders has been steadily increasing. Unskilled Lowland workers have been especially hard hit, leading to a growing anti-Highlander sentiment that erupted in riots last spring in Kapitalia.

Also taking aim at the government's policy toward refugees, Unsap claimed that few, if any, of the refugees were leaving Highland for political reasons, and that unemployment in Highland is the real reason for the influx of so-called refugees, most of whom are uneducated and illiterate.

Calling the government's attitude toward the problem irresponsible, Unsap also warned that an unlimited influx of non-Lowlanders would be a serious strain on the country's already inadequate social services, leading to further unrest among Lowland's unemployed.

Words with negative prefixes: **non- , un-, in-**

Lesson 6

Negative Prefixes: anti-, a-, dis-, mal-, mis-

In Lesson 5 we looked at negative prefixes that generally mean "not". In this lesson we will study some additional prefixes that have negative meanings.

anti- means against, opposite, or opposing.

antinuclear — opposing nuclear (energy or warfare)

● *Note: there is also a prefix* ante- *that means "before" or "earlier," but there are not many words in English with this prefix.*

a- means "not" or "without." It is also spelled **an-** when it is prefixed to a word that begins with a vowel.

a + political = apolitical — not political
a + archy = anarchy — without rule or government

dis- means "not," "apart from," "separate." It is also spelled **dif-** when prefixed to a word that begins with f, and in some cases, it is spelled **di-**. (And be careful that you don't confuse this with another prefix **di-**, which means "two.")

dis + agree = disagree — to not agree
dis + connect = disconnect — to separate a connection
dis + fuse = diffuse — to spread
dis + verge = diverge — to go in different directions

mal- means "bad," "badly," or "poor."

malnutrition — bad or poor nutrition

mis- also means "bad," but it can also mean "wrong" or "fail."

misfortune — bad fortune
miscalculate — to calculate wrongly
misfire — to fail to fire properly; "her gun misfired."

Exercises

A. Give a short definition of the "anti" words in the following sentences.

    1. The plane was shot down by antiaircraft guns. _____

    2. The Pro-Life group is in favor of antiabortion legislation.

        _____

    3. The two enemies could not hide their mutual antipathy.

        _____

    4. The Jewish delegation accused them of anti-Semitism.

        _____

    5. This new antitrust law is designed to encourage more competition.

        _____

    6. Synonyms are two words that have the same meaning. What are antonyms? (Notice the irregular spelling.)

        _____

B. Add the prefix a- or an- to the following list of bases. Check the unfamiliar words in your dictionary.

    _____ typical   _____ esthetic   _____ theism

    _____ archy   _____ sexual   _____ pathy

    _____ political   _____ nonymous   _____ aerobic

    _____ moral   _____ morphous   _____ symmetry

C. dis- can be prefixed to many words. Make a list of some that you know and compare your list with a friend, a teacher or the dictionary.

    _____

    _____

    _____

D. Below is a list of **mis-** and **mal-** words without their prefixes. See if you can match them with the proper prefix. You may make a few mismatches, but that's OK. Everybody makes mistakes.

    _____ behave   _____ content   _____ practice

    _____ judge   _____ manage   _____ fit

    _____ fortune   _____ function   _____ lead

    _____ nutrition   _____ guide   _____ adjusted

    _____ print   _____ place   _____ spell

E. Read the following story for general comprehension. Then read it more carefully and list the words with negative prefixes.

Candidates Disagree

Changeless claims lead in polls

In a nationally televised debate last night, the two leading candidates for president carried out a lively exchange that sharply differentiated their views on diverse issues.

I. M. Contra, speaking first, challenged the incumbent administration's record on environmental matters, claiming that the Conservative Union Party was "at best apathetic in its support of antipollution measures." Contra also attacked the administration's economic policies, claiming that mismanagement of the economy was bringing the nation close to "financial ruin and a state of unregulated anarchy."

In response, Dr. Changeless lashed out at Contra, calling him and his followers a "bunch of malcontents and misfits who would lead the country down the dusty road of disruption and disturbance." Dr. Changeless labelled Contra's Everyman Party the "AEP party or Anti-Everything Party," and charged that its leadership was "riddled with misguided and maladjusted atheists."

Contra responded to Changeless' attacks with sharp criticism of the administration's handling of the Robb Scandal, claiming that it was common knowledge that Robb had misappropriated funds and that the whole affair was a "malignant growth on the nation." He further claimed that the President had been misled and misinformed by his advisers. In Contra's words, "Robb should have been dismissed immediately." Contra closed his remarks with a final attack, saying that if Dr. Changeless were a medical doctor he would be guilty of malpractice and his patient, the republic, would soon be dead of governmental malnutrition.

In his closing statement, Dr. Changeless defended his administration and pointed to the divisive nature of the Everyman Party's campaign as a true indication of the amoral nature of the opposition party.

Claiming a 10-point lead in the latest polls, Dr. Changeless insisted that the voters would once again reject the opposition as unworthy to lead the country. "Remember the misgovernment of the 60's," he warned, "and don't make that mistake again. Your faith in my leadership is not misplaced." He concluded by saying that the opposition's tactics had misfired and that his Conservative Union Party would be victorious again.

Words with negative prefixes **dis-, mis-, mal-, a-, anti-**

Lesson 7

Quantity Prefixes: uni-, mono-, bi-, tri-, pan-, multi-, semi-, poly-, equi-

As you might guess, quantity prefixes indicate numbers, portions, or amounts of the bases to which they are affixed. You will encounter many of these prefixes in technical, scientific, and economic words that deal with measurements, comparisons, or descriptions of size or number. They do occur in everyday speech, however, and knowing their meanings can **multiply** your vocabulary.

Prefixes	Meanings
uni-	one
mono-/ mon-	one, single, or alone
bi-/ bin-	two, at intervals of two , or twice during . . .
tri-	three, occurring at intervals of three, occurring three times during . . .
pan-	all
multi-	many, much
	● *Note: use a hyphen before words beginning with* i, *multi-infection*
semi-	half, partial, occurring twice
	● *Note: hyphenate when the base begins with* i *or is capitalized*
poly-	more than one, much, many
equi-	equal, equally

Exercises

A. Use the meanings from the list above to help you define the words below or provide the word defined:

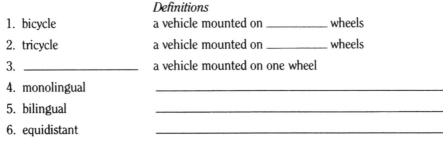

                                      Definitions

1. bicycle — a vehicle mounted on _____ wheels

2. tricycle — a vehicle mounted on _____ wheels

3. _____ — a vehicle mounted on one wheel

4. monolingual — _____

5. bilingual — _____

6. equidistant — _____

7. _____ having or speaking three languages

8. polylingual _____

9. panchromatic sensitive to _____ colors

10. _____ of only one color

11. _____ color another name for the French flag, which is blue, white and red in color

12. multilateral having _____ sides; involving _____ governments.

13. _____ involving two governments

14. _____ lateral affecting only one side or one government

15. semicolon _____

16. semiannual _____

17. _____ a room which is partially or half private

18. _____ half of a circle

19. _____ involving many nations

20. _____ all sides are the same

B. Match the prefixes **multi-**, **bi-**, **semi-** and **equi-** with an appropriate base. In some cases there are two possibilities.

media _____ _____

monthly _____ _____

skilled _____ _____

vitamin _____ _____

circular _____ _____

focal _____ _____

final _____ _____

millionaire _____ _____

purpose _____ _____

cultural _____ _____

precious _____ _____

centenary _____ _____

distant _____ _____

C. From the following advertisement list the words with quantity prefixes. Try to define them.

BECOME A POLYGLOT
WITH OUR HOME UNIVERSITY LANGUAGE COURSES

With our easy-to-follow manuals you can become bilingual in your own home!! Our materials are the perfected versions of courses used by the Diplomatic Service Institute.

In addition to the tapes and instructional manual you will receive a bimonthly multi-lingual newspaper with articles in French, Spanish, German, Italian, Russian, Mandarin, Swahili, and Japanese.

Our courses take the monotony out of language learning!

	WORD	MEANING
1.	_____	_____
2.	_____	_____
3.	_____	_____
4.	_____	_____
5.	_____	_____

D. Read the following selection first for general comprehension. Then read it for details and list all the words with quantity prefixes.

Pan-Equatorian Organization Meets

The Pan-Equatorian Organization opened its semi-annual meeting in Tropica today. On the agenda were proposals for a multimillion dollar hydro-electric station to serve the tri-state area of Tropica, Savanna, and Occidentia, and a request for funding of a solar-powered station. The station would be located in Savanna, equidistant from Tropica and Occidentia.

A subcommittee on the development of the Pan-Equatorian transportation network presented a plan for a monorail service. The service, to be called Pan-Equatorian Transport, or PET for short, will be the first low-cost, trans-Equatorian transportation system. This will help to unify the three nations on a multitude of levels in addition to providing transportation.

The subcommittee on multilingual issues pushed for a ruling that all official documents be trilingual: French, English, and the local language; and that universities now require all graduates to be bilingual—native language plus French or English. The education subcommittee unveiled plans for a Polytechnic Institute to be established in Savanna. The Institute will be the first cooperative educational venture undertaken by the three Equatorian nations.

The literacy subcommittee reported that the recent biennial survey of literacy in the three nations has shown that illiteracy has been reduced by 10 per cent.

Discussion of bilateral trade agreements with the EEC was suspended until later.

Dr. Jeanne Shagari advocates solar power for Savanna at Tropica meeting today.   MJP

Words with quantity prefixes:

Lesson 8
Verb Prefixes and Suffixes: en-, -en, be-, -ify, -ize, -ate

One common way of showing that a word is a verb, is to prefix or suffix it with **en**. The meaning of **en** is, in general, to make or create. Sometimes it intensifies (makes stronger) the meaning of the base.

en- is frequently prefixed to bases that are nouns or verbs:

   enact- to put something (especially a law) into action.

If the base begins with a **b** or **p**, **en-** is spelled **em-** : **empower** — to give power to somebody.

-en is frequently suffixed to adjectives of quality or dimension:

   shorten — to make shorter
   sharpen — to make sharper

● *Note: there is also the past participle inflection -en, which is a different kind of affix:* break — broke — broken.

be- as a prefix has an intensifying effect on the base form. It can also mean "to cause to . . ."

   belittle — to speak of something as unimportant.
   becloud — to cause something to be difficult to see or understand.

-ify, **-ate** and **-ize** are common verb suffixes that also mean, in general, "to make." There is no easy way of knowing which suffix is attached to which base. The combinations have to be memorized.

● *Note: in British English -ize is usually spelled -ise, although Americans also spell some words like* televise *with an* s. *Also note that a few words like* execute *or* prosecute *take a* -ute *suffix instead of* -ate.

These **ify**,**-ate**, and-**ize** verbs are easily turned into nouns by adding -**ion** and making a few spelling changes. Note that -**ify** verbs usually add -**ication**.

| identify | — | identification | realize | — | realization |
| investigate | — | investigation | contribute | — | contribution |

Exercises

A.   Some of the following bases are prefixed with en- or em-, and some are suffixed with -en. Try to use the correct affix.

soft	wide	trust	dorse
danger	close	loose	courage
able	gage	dure	counter
deep	bright	force	hance
ploy	weak	brace	gulf

B.   Use the words below in a sentence where they would be appropriate.

beware	beclouded	behooves	belittle	betrayed
bereaved	bemoaned	bedevilled	bewildering	besieged

1.   He _____ his friends and told the police where they were hiding.

2.   This is a complex, _____ situation. I am confused.

3.   The _____ parents _____ the loss of their only son.

4.   Many problems have _____ the latest attempt to launch a satellite. The project may
      be cancelled.

5.   It _____ us to buy now. The price will never be lower.

6.   _____ of the dog; it bites.

7.   Don't _____ the idea unless you have a better one.

8.   The city was _____ for months before it finally surrendered.

9.   The issue was clear, but I'm afraid they have _____ it.

C.   In these sentences use either the **-ate** or **-ize** verb suffix to make the verb form.

1.   The demonstrators will _____ tomorrow.

2.   The immigrants _____ mostly from the Far East.

3.   The Nationalist party wants to _____ the steel industry.

4.   As a dramatist, he _____ man's struggle with God and the devil.

5.   Two assassins _____ the minister yesterday.

6.   A private investigator will _____ the matter.

7.   Negotiators have _____ a peaceful settlement.

8.   If she's a university graduate, where did she _____ from?

9.   The operators refused to _____ the equipment.

10. Terrorists have _____ the entire area.

11. We should never make this legal. If it is _____, the problem will worsen.

12. At this time speculation is dangerous. Therefore, I refuse to _____.

D.   Put the following base forms in the proper column. Note that there is a word **certificate**, but it is
      a noun.

ident-	class-	capital-	simpl-	civil-	intens-
activ-	fals-	equal-	appropri-	ideall-	final-
loc-	uni-	toler	differenti-	romantic-	cert-

-ify	-ate	-ize
_____	_____	_____
_____	_____	_____
_____	_____	_____
_____	_____	_____
_____	_____	_____
_____		_____

E. Read the following article once through for general comprehension. Then read it again and list all the words with verb prefixes and suffixes. Note that although a word may have a verb affix, it may also have a noun suffix, following the verb affix. For example, drama<u>tiz</u>ation, from drama<u>tize</u>. List all the words that contain a verb affix.

Courtroom Drama Intensifies

Doble calls Boss Solo Drug King

The trial of Juan Solo continued today in San Tomaso, Nova Mundo, as the prosecution, attempting to strengthen its case, brought forth a new witness to testify against Solo, who is accused of operating a huge drug empire that produces and distributes cocaine throughout central Caribea.

The witness, Julio Doble, identified Solo as the ringleader of a gang of drug dealers that for the past ten years has terrorized the provincial city of Los Gatos, located in the remote northeastern part of Andea. Doble, characterizing Solo as the "Andean Godfather," claimed that Solo had managed to centralize a chain of growers, processors, and distributors from his headquarters in Los Gatos.

Upon cross-examination by the defense, the witness, who had immigrated to Nova Mundo and become a naturalized citizen in 1986, admitted that he had falsified information on his naturalization papers and had covered up an arrest and conviction in 1981 for embezzling funds from the First Andean Bank, where he had been employed in the 1970's. Apparently, Doble also lost a large sum of money by speculating in real estate.

Bewildered by the defense's examination, the besieged witness also admitted that two years ago he had been investigated by the Nova Mundo Drug Enforcement Agency.

The defense appealed to the jury to recognize the witness as a questionable character, and stated that his testimony should be classified as simply that of "an informant whose only purpose is to betray Solo, a former ally in the drug world." Arguing that the defense was doing nothing more than trying to assassinate the character of the witness in order to frighten further witnesses, the federal attorney vowed to continue to prosecute the case with additional witnesses when the trial resumes tomorrow.

***Words with verb prefixes and suffixes* en-, -en, be-, -ify, -ize, -ate:**

Lesson 9

Noun Suffixes: -ance/-ence, -ity, -hood, -ship, -ness

Suffixes are attached to the end of a base, and they do two things. They carry some meaning, and they show what kind of word they are a part of. For example, in Lesson 3 we saw that the -er suffix means "one who," and it also shows that the word is a noun.

In this lesson we will look at some other suffixes that form nouns. (In other lessons we will study adjective, adverb, and verb suffixes.) In general, the noun suffixes in this lesson mean the "condition, state of being, or quality" of the base they are affixed to. For example, if you have **security**, your condition is **secure**. Often when these suffixes are affixed to a base ending in a vowel, the final vowel is either changed or dropped, as it is in **insurance**.

-ance/-ence has these variant forms: -ancy/-ency and -acy.

> insure + ance = insurance
> intelligent + ence = intelligence
> president + ency = presidency
> occupant + ancy = occupancy
> democrat + acy = democracy

-ity is occasionally spelled -ety.

> secure + ity = security
> soci + ity = society

-hood can mean "condition, state, or quality," but it can also mean "a group of."

> state + hood = statehood — the condition of being a state
> neighbor + hood = neighborhood — a place where a group of neighbors live.
> brother + hood = brotherhood — either a group of brothers or the quality of being like brothers.

-ship, in addition to meaning "condition, state, or quality," can also mean "status, rank, or office."

> leader + ship = leadership (quality)
> professor + ship = professorship (rank)

-**ness** means "condition, state, or quality," and it is frequently suffixed to adjectives that already have an adjective suffix.

> kind + ness = kindness — the quality of being kind
> careful + ness = carefulness — the quality of being careful.
> divisive + ness = divisiveness — the quality of being devisive
> sleepy + ness = sleepiness — the state of being sleepy
> drunken + ness = drunkenness — the condition or state of being drunk

Exercises.

A. Rewrite the following words to see if you can guess which affix to use: -ance, -ence, -ancy, -ency, -acy.

intelligent	_____	assist	_____
assure	_____	dissident	_____
president	_____	democrat	_____
conspire	_____	insist	_____
disturb	_____	prefer	_____
candidate	_____	illiterate	_____
agent	_____	differ	_____
disappear	_____	confer	_____
resident	_____	independent	_____
_____			

B. Add the suffix -ity to these words (watch the spelling) and use the word in one of the sentences.

secure	active
captive	equal
similar	simple
familiar	human

1. There is a great _____ between the flags of Australia and New Zealand.

2. When will _____ ever achieve universal peace?

3. I have no _____ with that subject.

4. The prisoner was kept in _____ for two years.

5. "Our goal is _____ and brotherhood," he said.

6. The _____ of her life style contrasts with the complexity of her ideas.

7. Observers reported that there was no unusual _____ along the border today.

8. _____ will be tight when the President visits the provincial capital.

C.   Fill in the blanks with a noun form of the <u>underlined</u> adjective.

1.   The rate of change has been <u>steady.</u>

Its _____ is very assuring.

2.   The comments are <u>unworthy</u> of response.

The _____ of your comments is disappointing.

3.   His response was <u>correct.</u>

The _____ of his response was not surprising.

4.   The night was <u>still.</u>

The _____ of the night was pleasant.

5.   You were very <u>kind</u>.

Your _____ is much appreciated.

6.   The situation was <u>hopeless.</u>

The _____ of the situation was obvious.

7.   One <u>careless</u> act can create a disaster.
The disaster was caused by _____.

8.   She was trying to be <u>helpful.</u>

Her _____ was sincere.

9.   Don't be <u>foolish.</u> They won't tolerate your _____.

10. He was always very <u>busy</u> but <u>careful.</u> His _____ and _____ helped him build

a good _____.

D.   Add either -ship or -hood.

1.   He has citizen_____ in two countries.
2.   Alaska achieved state_____in 1959.
3.   We live in a quiet neighbor_____.
4.   Her leader_____ was inspiring.
5.   Throughout his child_____ he was often sick.
6.   I am against all forms of censor _____.
7.   The craftsman _____ in this jewelry is unequaled anywhere.
8.   This country has lived under a dictator _____ for too many years.
9.   This union is called the Brother _____ of Mine Workers.
10. Nehru's statesman _____ earned him the respect of people everywhere.

E.   Read the following article and list the words with the noun suffixes we have studied in this lesson.

Leader of Independence Movement Dies

Condolences and tributes continued to pour into the capital of Territoria, as the citizens began an official, three-day mourning for the death of R.J. Lee, who passed away peacefully at his residence Tuesday morning.

Born and brought up in a poverty-stricken neighborhood in the provincial city of Interioria, Lee first gained national recognition when he led the Brotherhood of Mine Workers in a successful strike and a series of protests against expatriate mine ownership.

In the 1930s he served his political apprenticeship as a District Representative to the legislature during the colonial administration. His political experiences, however, turned him against the government, and together with W.W. Hong, he founded the Unity Party and began to develop its policy of civil disobedience.

In the closing years of the colonial administration, Lee came into prominence as a leader of the independence movement, and in 1955, as a champion of democracy, he announced his candidacy for Prime Minister with his now-famous "Equality and Opportunity" address, delivered at the closing session of the National Legislature.

Elected as Prime Minister of Territoria, Lee led the country in its first few years of nationhood. Although noted for his fairness and his tolerance of minority opinion, he was frequently criticized by the independent press for operating an undeclared dictatorship.

In 1962 he was elected to the presidency of Territoria. As President, Lee achieved an international reputation for his statesmanship and his life-long adherence to non-violence. He helped establish the Annual Conference of Nonaligned Nations.

Over the next few days official delegations from dozens of countries will assemble in the capital to attend the final ceremonies for the ex-President. He will be buried Friday in the National Cemetery.

Words with noun suffixes **-ance/-ence, -acy, -ency, -ity, -hood, -ship, -ness:**

Lesson 10

Noun Suffixes: -ion, -ment, -ism, -age, -dom

In the previous lesson we studied noun suffixes that refer to condition, state, or quality. The suffixes in this lesson are similar but can also have an "active" meaning.

-ion, which usually indicates "an act, process, or condition," is sometimes spelled -tion, -sion, -ation and -ition.

>   act + ion = action
>   nutri + tion = nutrition
>   suspen + sion = suspension
>   domin + ation = domination
>   compet + ition = competition

-ment, which can mean "action, product, or state," is a common suffix.

>   govern + ment = government

-ism, can refer to action: **terror + ism = terrorism**
or to qualities: **hero + ism = heroism**
or to a doctrine or principle: **commun + ism = communism**

-age can mean "an action or condition": **marry + age = marriage**
or "a collection or mass": **post + age = postage.**

-dom is the only suffix in this group that doesn't refer to action. It is not a common suffix, and it usually means "a field of interest or action."

>   king + dom = kingdom

In a few cases it can refer to a condition:

>   free + dom = freedom.

Exercises

A. We have seen one form or another of all these -ion suffixed words in previous lessons. All of these nouns can be changed into verbs. Write the verb form next to the noun.

investigation	_____	pollution	_____
location	_____	disruption	_____
prevention	_____	rejection	_____
prosecution	_____	indication	_____
collision	_____	conclusion	_____
confirmation	_____	organization	_____
identification	_____	presentation	_____
demonstration	_____	provision	_____
acclamation	_____	graduation	_____
contribution	_____	cooperation	_____
immigration	_____	recognition	_____
opposition	_____	election	_____
eruption	_____	operation	_____
administration	_____	explosion	_____

What did you notice about nouns that end with - **sion**?

B. Most of the words in this list take a -**ment** suffix, but a few do not. Add the -**ment** suffix to the appropriate words, and put an X beside the words that do not take a -**ment** suffix.

appoint	_____	develop	_____
announce	_____	require	_____
expect	_____	contribute	_____
manage	_____	compose	_____
govern	_____	establish	_____
state	_____	move	_____
criticize	_____		

C. All of the -ism words below can be found in one form or another in readings 1-8. A person who is involved in an -ism is usually an -ist. In the list below, only two "people" words do not have an -ist ending. Can you find them?

terrorism _____   conservatism _____

tourism _____   nationalism _____

idealism _____   socialism _____

activism _____   criticism _____

capitalism _____   colonialism _____

classicism _____   opportunism _____

D. Complete the following sentences using -dom and -age suffixes. Most of the words will require -age, which is much more common than -dom.

1. The ship was wrecked. Some of the _____ came ashore.

2. All the media covered the event. The _____ was very complete.

3. They shot many feet of film. The film _____ was examined closely.

4. She is a star. She achieved _____ at an early age.

5. The river was polluted by sewers. The _____ came from the city.

6. It cost a lot to post the letter. The _____ was very high.

7. We are free. We have _____ at last!

8. It is the same size as a pack of cigarettes. It comes in a small _____.

9. An auto can carry things. It used to be called a horseless _____.

10. The freezer broke and the meat spoiled. The restaurant was not insured against food _____ .

11. He is a martyr. He achieved _____ by dying for his country.

12. They were bored by the speech. Their _____ was easy to see.

13. The two movie stars were married last year. Their _____ lasted only a year.

14. He had four bags. The _____ allowance was only three bags. (He had too much luggage).

15. Some articles will be broken. You should allow for 10% _____.

16. She's a stock broker. Her business is a _____.

E.   Read the following article first for general comprehension. Then read it more closely and list all the words with suffixes we have studied in this lesson.

HAMAD III, LATE KING OF BURANIA

Assassination Investigation

The normally peaceful Monarchy of Burania is slowly returning to business-as-usual after the shocking assassination last Tuesday of King Hamad III. Shops and offices that remained closed yesterday, began to open today as the government issued a declaration that the administration of the Kingdom would not be disrupted by terrorism.

Although positive identification of the assassin has not been made, an announcement from the Ministry of Information has tentatively linked the assassin, who was shot and killed on the spot by the king's bodyguards, to the little-known Burania Freedom Fighters faction.

Meanwhile, an anonymous phone caller, claiming to be a member of the outlawed ODN (Organization for Democratic Nationalism) praised the dead assassin saying, "He has attained martyrdom, and others will follow in his footsteps."

The Central Intelligence Department's investigation of the murder is continuing under the direction of Major General Adam. According to Adam, studies of television film footage have revealed the possible presence of a second assassin who may have fired a rifle from the rooftop of the Hotel Elegan. The figure on the rooftop lends credence to the speculation that the King may have been hit by a bullet a split-second before the terrorist bomb exploded in his open carriage. The Monarch, who was being driven to a reception at the Palace was apparently killed by the explosion of the package bomb hurled by the assailant. The vehicle's wreckage is being examined for the presence of the rifle slugs, and it is expected that the results of an autopsy on the King will be released later today.

A statement this morning from the King's son, Prince Mahad, appealed to the citizens of Burania to remain calm. "Their aim is disruption and anarchy," he said, referring to the murderers, "but we must work for the continuation of my father, the king's peaceful and progressive rule."

Words with noun suffixes -ion, ment, -ism, -age, -dom:

Lesson 11

Adjective Suffixes: -able, -less, -al, -en

The suffix **-able** means "can or able to . . ." and the suffix **-less** means "to be without or lacking."

-able is also spelled **-ible**. There are no simple rules to know which spelling is used. You may need to consult a dictionary. In general, however, bases that are complete words add **-able**. Also notice that if the word ends in e, sometimes the e is dropped. If the word ends in **-ate**, the **-ate** is usually dropped and **-able** is added.

> return + able = returnable — can be returned
> incred + ible = incredible — cannot be believed
> believ(e) + able = believable — can be believed
> demonstr(ate) + able = demonstrable — can be demonstrated

-less means "without."

> **hopeless** — without hope

-al means "related to or characterized by."

> **political** — relating to politics

-en means "made of or resembling." Be careful that you don't confuse this suffix with the past participle inflection (**break, broke, broken**) or the verb suffix **-en** (**sharpen, widen, lengthen**).

> **wooden** — made of wood

Exercises

A. It is not easy to choose between **-able** and **-ible**. Try adding the suffix to these bases.

believe	_____	response	_____
permiss	_____	tolerate	_____
receive	_____	reason	_____
question	_____	predict	_____
advise	_____	defense	_____
poss-	_____	consider	_____
accept	_____	cred-	_____
measure	_____	manage	_____
operate	_____	defend	_____

B. Create a new word using the Italicized word in the following sentences:

1. He is a very ordinary person. It's not easy to *recognize* him. He's not easily _____.

2. Although the noise is rather loud I can *toler*ate it. It is _____.

3. Natural gas has no *odor* and no *color* and cannot be *detect*ed. Since it is _____ and _____, an odor has been added to make it _____.

4. Everyone *like*s her; she has a _____ personality.

5. Thank you for a very _____ evening. We *enjoy*ed ourselves a lot.

6. This card table is _____. If you *collaps*e the legs it can be stored behind the door.

7. A discussion or meeting that produced no results or *fruit* can be called _____.

8. This plastic tube can be bent or *flex*ed easily; it is _____.

9. There is no *hope* for this patient; his situation is _____.

10. At one time it was the *fashion*, or it was _____ for men to wear ruffled shirts.

C. Add the appropriate adjectival suffix to each word and keep in mind that those with the suffix -en generally mean "made of," while those ending in -al mean "related to or characterized by . . ."

1. It is just an old wood_____ box, but it is special to me because my grandfather built it when he was just a boy.

2. The doctor recommended that the patient be hospitalized since he was showing suicid_____ tendencies.

3. A dentist is also called an or_____ surgeon since his work is related to the mouth.

4. This course is not required; it is option_____.

5. There were many colorful flor_____ arrangements at the ceremony.

6. The dining room table is egg-shaped, or ov_____.

7. She survived the cold because she was wearing heavy wool_____ clothes and a therm_____ jacket.

8. This is a gold_____ opportunity!

9. The reception is form_____; you should wear a suit and tie.

10. The Indians made good use of their environment to produce their everyday necessities such as earth _____ ware pottery.

D. Match the adjectives with the most appropriate nouns. (Suggestion: Choose a noun. Then read the list of adjectives and find the most appropriate one.)

1. _____ tropical   a. animal
2. _____ woolen   b. table
3. _____ classical   c. action
4. _____ defenseless   d. job
5. _____ legal   e. island
6. _____ golden   f. analysis
7. _____ thankless   g. music
8. _____ unbelievable   h. ring
9. _____ wooden   i. sweater
10. _____ financial   j. story

E. Read the following article first for general comprehension. Then read it more closely and list all the words with the suffixes we have studied in this lesson.

Undetectable Explosives Now Illegal

The government of Crovenia today decreed that all plastic explosives will now include an impurity, making them easily detectable by new airport security screening devices. Until now the odorless, non-magnetic material has managed to elude all security systems, leaving guards helpless in trying to stop terrorism in the airline industry.

Plastic explosives are made of very flexible material that is easily concealable. These qualities make it virtually impossible to detect the explosives, leaving the airline industry defenseless against a determined terrorist.

A decision to require the implantation of recognizable impurities was made following a recent colloquium on new security systems and devices. Present technology is powerless to identify the plastic explosives in pure form. Requirements that plastics production now include an identifiable substance will help security teams.

The explosive material is one of Crovenia's most profitable exports, although its production has become more controversial with increased world-wide terrorism.

Words with adjective suffixes -able, -less, -al, -en:

Lesson 12

Adjective Suffixes: -ful, -y, -ous, -ary

Like the adjective suffixes -able and -less, the suffix -ful is easy to define. It means that something is "full of or filled with" the base.   -ful can also have a more general meaning of "having the quality of, or the tendency to . . ." The suffixes -y and -ous are similar in meaning to -ful. Here are some examples of -ful, -y, -ous:

peaceful	dirty	famous
successful	cloudy	dangerous
faithful	salty	various
purposeful	sleepy	serious

● *Note: There is another -y suffix which is used to mean something small or dear. For example: **kitty, daddy, mommy**.*

The **-ary** suffix means "connected with or engaged in." Remember that there is also a noun suffix **-ary**, which is also spelled **-ory** (see Lesson 4). Here are some words with **-ary** as an adjective suffix: **ordinary, secondary, budgetary.**

Exercises

A.   Give a short explanation of the following phrases.

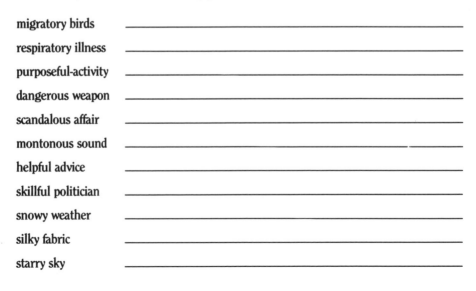

migratory birds   _____

respiratory illness   _____

purposeful-activity   _____

dangerous weapon   _____

scandalous affair   _____

montonous sound   _____

helpful advice   _____

skillful politician   _____

snowy weather   _____

silky fabric   _____

starry sky   _____

B.   Provide an appropriate suffix for the underlined words. Check your work in the dictionary.

1.   Economists are <u>hope</u>_____ that the current fiscal year will end with a lower rate of inflation than last year.

2.   Conservative investors are wary of speculation and prefer to use caution or to be <u>cauti</u>_____.

3.   The development of communication systems has brought <u>revolution</u>_____ changes to the 20th century world.

4.   He is an expert chef; he learned his <u>culin</u>_____ skills at the best restaurants in Paris.

5.   Please be very <u>care</u>_____ not to wake the baby when you enter.

6.   To prevent the spread of disease we must take <u>precaution</u>_____ measures.

7.   Measles is an <u>infecti</u>_____ disease.

8.   If you want to lose weight you should avoid <u>greas</u>_____ and <u>starch</u>_____ foods.

9.   It is too <u>fogg</u>_____ to drive right now.

10. She owns a <u>luxuri</u>_____ house at the seaside.

C.   Transform the following words into adjectives by applying the correct suffixes:

ridicule	_____		string	_____
oil	_____		faith	_____
thank	_____		envy	_____
scare	_____		ice	_____
greed	_____		melody	_____
ambition	_____		pearl	_____
thought	_____		second	_____
inflation	_____		purpose	_____
fiction	_____		vision	_____

What did you notice about the spelling of words that end with **y** to which the suffix **-OUS** is attached?

D.   Many -y suffixes are used to describe weather conditions. After the following words write "W," to indicate a "weather" word.

snowy	_____	grassy	_____	sunny	_____
stony	_____	foggy	_____	rocky	_____
windy	_____	dusty	_____	sandy	_____
muddy	_____	icy	_____	rainy	_____
chilly	_____	hazy	_____	smoggy	_____
salty	_____	smoky	_____	cloudy	_____
milky	_____	hilly	_____	misty	_____

E. Read the following story for general comprehension. Then list the **-ful, -y, -ous,** and **-ary** words.

Disastrous Earthquake in Kosharam

A disastrous earthquake in the mountainous region of Kosharam has killed hundreds and completely destroyed many villages built on the rocky slopes of the Altaya Mountains. Survivors are staying in temporary housing provided by voluntary relief organizations.

The primary shock waves from the powerful earthquake registered 7.2 on the Richter scale. It occurred Sunday morning when most people were at home. Hundreds of buildings collapsed, killing or trapping the unwary residents. Most of the ordinary houses had been built long before the establishment of the Regulatory Building Commission, and therefore they did not have sturdy, earthquake-proof foundations.

Several poor neighborhoods in the hilly terrain surrounding the city of Kashkar were destroyed by landslides. Dangerous landslide conditions had been created by the previous week's exceptionally rainy weather, and the quake's first jolt caused the sandy, rain-soaked soil to slip down the hillsides.

Secondary shock waves were also reported to have struck the region Monday evening, but fortunately no disastrous results were recorded.

Generous donations have been pouring in from thoughtful citizens everywhere. The parliamentary session opened Monday with a moment of silence to honor those who had perished and was followed by an immediate resolution to grant financial assistance and help from the military forces for the stricken region.

Words with **-ful, -y, -ous, -ary** *suffixes:*

Lesson 13

Adjective Suffixes: -ish, -ic, -ive

These suffixes are frequently used to mean "having a tendency to, related to, or characteristic of" the base to which they are joined.

reddish brown — a brown color that has some red
childish behavior — behavior (in an adult) that is like a child
destructive storm — a storm that destroys things (causes destruction)
economic report — a report that is related to the economy

● *Note: Be careful of the difference between economic and economical, which means "not expensive to operate."*

Exercises

A.   Try to guess the right suffix. There are four -ic, four -ish, and three -ive suffixes in the sentences below.

1.   The soldier was given a medal for his hero_____ behavior.

2.   She has a schizophren_____ personality.

3.   We appreciate construct_____ comments but not destruct_____ ones.

4.   Her eyes are brown_____ .

5.   The comedian's boy_____ , com_____ behavior makes people laugh.

6.   No one can say that he is self_____; he always puts others first.

7.   The artist's creat_____ work was not appreciated in her lifetime.

8.   How could anyone make such a fool_____ mistake?!!

9.   People with ulcers should not eat acid_____ fruits.

B. Use the list below to fill in the blanks in the sentences.

collective	fantastic	brackish	organic
sluggish	metallic	conclusive	fortyish
girlish	microscopic	geometric	

1. The aluminum pot gave the coffee a _____ taste.

2. In the hot, sweltering summer temperatures, we were too_____ to play any active sports.

3. _____ organisms are very, very small.

4. The judge said there was not enough _____ evidence to find the defendant guilty.

5. Don't let her _____ appearance fool you; she is really_____ .

6. Even though centuries old, the Turkish kilims' _____ designs fit in well with many modern decors.

7. Believing that synthetic chemical fertilizers are harmful, _____ farmers use only natural fertilizers.

8. The view from the mountaintop is _____ .

9. Water that is somewhat salty is _____ water.

10. _____ bargaining enabled the workers to negotiate for better working conditions.

C. Complete the following with an appropriate adjective. In some cases partial spellings have been given to help you. Use your dictionary if necessary.

1. Her eyes are not really a deep or pure blue; they are more of a _____ish blue.

2. Before a storm the sea often changes to a _____ish color.

3. A woman who is not beautiful but who attracts attention can be called att_____ive.

4. If I tickle or touch you in sensitive places and you laugh, you are t_____lish.

5. Many people do not believe in UFO's (unidentified flying objects) because there is no scien_____c evidence of their existence.

6. If you want to emphasize something, you can underline it or use ital_____ script to make it stand out.

7. Although inches, feet and yards are still commonly used in the USA, the met_____ system is taught in the public school and is often used in science and technology.

8. To straighten the child's crooked teeth the dentist recommended correct_____ braces.

9. To take this course you must have a bas_____ knowledge of the principles of accounting.

D. Give the noun and verb forms of the following adjectives.

ADJECTIVE	NOUN	VERB
dramatic	drama	dramatize
magnetic		

telephonic _____ _____

systematic _____ _____

explosive _____ _____

creative _____ _____

defensive _____ _____

conclusive _____ _____

disruptive _____ _____

progressive _____ _____

decisive _____ _____

productive _____ _____

E. Some nationalities and languages end with an -ish suffix and can be used as nouns or adjectives. Can you name some?

_____ _____ _____

_____ _____ _____

_____ _____ _____

F. Read the following passage first for general comprehension. Then read it for details and list all the -ish, -ic, and -ive suffixes.

Dramatic Rescue at Island Park

The sleepy Wabasset River town Placidboro, usually an idyllic spot year-round, was awakened from its slumber Sunday morning to find that massive ice blocks had broken loose from the river's frozen surface. The broken ice flowed downriver to Island Park, where it piled up and began a relentless destruction of the island. Fortunately, no one was hurt, although damage to property was extensive.

Eli Sharp, caretaker of Island Park Casino, had been stranded on the island since the ice began breaking up at around 2:00 Sunday morning. With much of the island covered by thick chunks of ice, Sharp was forced to take refuge on the roof of the casino building.

Called to the scene by Sharp's frantic wife, the Placidboro Public Safety Department attempted to rescue Sharp by motorboat, but despite the heroic efforts of the crew, the normally sluggish river was choked with floating ice, and they were unable to reach the island.

Within an hour, however, a police helicopter from nearby Metropol picked Sharp from the roof of the Casino in a dramatic rescue operation, just as the destructive force of water and ice began to destroy the Casino. Sharp, unharmed but slightly feverish from exposure to the cold, was transferred to the hospital for observation.

Casino owner Frank Chance looked on helplessly as his classic wooden structure was slowly destroyed. Asked if he would rebuild, Chance replied that for the moment he was simply grateful for the unselfish efforts of the rescuers, and that he was thankful that his trusted employee Sharp was alive.

Chance went on to praise the decisive action of Police Chief Standish and the rescuers. "They were terrific," said Chance.

Words with -ish, -ic, *and* -ive *suffixes:*

Lesson 14

Adverb Suffixes: -ly, -ward, -wise

The most active and common adverb suffix is **-ly**. It can be added to a long list of words (mostly adjectives) to make them into adverbs — words that modify adjectives or verbs. The adverb ending is often added to words that already have a suffix, but notice that the adverb suffix always comes last. Note the order of affixes in **internationally**, which has four affixes:

inter-	nat	-ion	-al	-ly
prefix	base	noun suffix	adjective suffix	adverb suffix

There are some spelling problems with **-ly**.

1. In a word that ends in a **y** preceded by a consonant, change the **y** to **i**.
    happy + ly = happily

2. In an adjective that ends in **-ble, -ple, -tle, -dle**, drop the **-le**:
    possible + ly = possibly

3. With adjectives that end in **-ic**, add **-al** before **-ly**:
    basic + ly = basically

4. With adjectives ending in "silent" **-e**, keep the **-e**:
    extreme + ly = extremely

5. With adjectives ending in **l**, keep the **l**.
    careful + ly = carefully

● *Note: A few words suffixed with -ly are normally adjectives: **lively, friendly, neighborly, lovely, lonely**.*

-ward is usually suffixed to words of direction. The list is short. Note that an **-s** can be added to the end of most of these words with no change in meaning.

toward(s)	backward(s)
downward(s)	forward(s)
upward(s)	homeward(s)
inward(s)	onward(s)
outward(s)	skyward

-wise is suffixed to a few words to make them into adverbs:

    lengthwise   clockwise   crosswise

It is quite common nowadays to add the -wise suffix to nouns. However, this is not yet a fully acceptable practice. The adverbial expression means "pertaining to . . ." For example: **Moneywise,** we've got to be careful. We're almost broke!

    moneywise   marketwise   timewise   budgetwise

● *Note: This adverbial form should not be confused with the more accepted adjectival phrase meaning "well informed about . . ." For example:* Budgetwise, *Joe is hopeless. He just isn't* budget wise.

Exercises

A.   Below are some adjectives that we have seen before. Rewrite the word with the -ly suffix, spelling carefully.

federal	_____	responsible	_____
automatic	_____	national	_____
apparent	_____	appropriate	_____
intelligent	_____	immediate	_____
normal	_____	peaceful	_____
political	_____	successful	_____
ideal	_____	clever	_____
environmental	_____	independent	_____
conservative	_____	democratic	_____
illegal	_____	fair	_____
financial	_____	progressive	_____
steady	_____	secure	_____

B.   Write the adverb form in the following sentences.

1. His progress is steady. He is progressing _____.

2. Active participation is necessary. Please participate _____.

3. She's always fair. She treats people _____.

4. Be sure it is secure. Tie it _____.

5. He is a successful businessman. He manages his business _____.

6. I will take a conservative view. I will act _____.

7. The situation is normal. Everything is proceeding _____.

8. She is known everywhere in the nation. She is a _____ known person.

9. The problem is apparent. _____ this is the problem.

10. We are concerned about the environment. We are _____ concerned citizens.

11. Their reaction was immediate. They reacted _____.

12. Let's seek a peaceful solution. Let's solve the problem _____.

13. That was an illegal act. He did it _____ .

14. It's an automatic rifle. It fires _____ .

15. We need an appropriate response. We need to respond _____ .

C. Match the phrases on the left with a phrase on the right.

1. Illegally printed money is _____   a. in a good location.

2. A democratically ruled nation is _____   b. interesting and entertaining.

3. A financially independent person is _____   c. an important point in time.

4. An ideally situated home is _____   d worthless.

5. A federally funded project is _____   e. usually peaceful.

6. A steadily increasing debt is _____   f. for the purpose of maintaining power.

7. A normally idyllic place is _____   g. a country with free elections.

8. A cleverly told story is _____   h. not in need of money.

9. A politically motivated action is _____   i. growing larger every day.

10. A critically decisive moment is _____   j. one which receives government money.

D. Use the words below in the sentences. Use each word only once.

lengthwise	downward	skyward	inward
budgetwise	forward	outward	homeward
toward	backward		

1. The price of the food is dropping. It's going _____ .

2. The rocket roared _____ .

3. The city is slowly expanding _____ .

4. Place it the long way. Place it _____ .

5. We're not making progress. We're going _____ .

6. Most of the traffic leaving the city in the evening is _____ bound to the suburbs.

7. _____ , we can't do it. It will cost too much.

8. We are moving _____ a solution.

9. We were moving _____ . Then we came to a complete stop.

10. The psychiatrist said, "I want you to look _____ and get in touch with your real feelings."

E. Read the following article quickly and completely. Then read it again, looking for adverb suffixes.

Environmentalists
Plead Urgently for Solutions

At the conclusion of a three-day conference in Nova Arkansk, an internationally known group of environmental scientists released a dramatically worded statement on the "greenhouse" effect. The scientists issued a warning that the increasing use of fossil fuels and the release of chemicals into the atmosphere will invariably lead to steadily rising temperature levels and climatic changes that will create enormous disruptions globally, including a rise in ocean levels and flooding of coastal areas.

The burning of fossil fuels directly results in an increase in carbon dioxide. The increase in carbon dioxide, which traps the sun's rays in the lower atmosphere, indirectly causes the temperature increase.

On the one hand, with more carbon dioxide in the atmosphere, agricultural productivity will increase significantly. Carbon dioxide enhances photosynthesis in green plants and decreases moisture requirements. Accordingly, some nations may benefit from climatic changes; others, principally developing nations, will be sorely pressed to cope with the changes. Agricultural conditions worldwide will almost certainly be significantly altered. Environmental and economic systems potentially will be disrupted.

The report also stressed the negative effects, politically and economically, on densely populated coastal regions, especially those of Asia and the Pacific region. Low-lying islands may be partially or even completely inundated forcing thousands of islanders to leave. Mainland coastal areas, which would also be severely affected, contain nearly one-third of the world's population.

Additionally, much of the world's great rice-growing area in Asia could be drastically affected as increasingly brackish water would be devastating to the variety of rice currently grown in these areas.

The scientists called for a multinational effort by developing and developed nations to work together immediately toward a meaningful solution. The report concluded by stating that priority must be given to reducing the use of fossil fuels, and preserving and expanding forests which absorb carbon dioxide. "We must look forward," the scientists said, "and keep our vision straight ahead to the future. We cannot delay another year, or civilization in the 21st century will slip backward into turmoil and chaos."

Words with adverb suffixes -ly, -ward, -wise:

Lesson 15

Position Prefixes: pre-, post-, inter-, intro-/intra-, extro-/extra-

In Lessons 5-7 we studied negative and quantity prefixes. In this lesson we will look at prefixes that modify the base word by giving information about the location of the base in space or time.

Preposition is a good example to help you remember this group of **prefixes.**

Pre- and **post-** are very common prefixes that mean "before" and "after." These prefixes can be attached to many bases: A hyphen is used if the combination is somewhat unusual, or if the base begins with a capital letter. And if the base begins with the letter e, the **pre-** prefix is hyphenated.

      pretrial — before the trial (in time)
      postwar — after the war (in time)
      pre-Colombian — before Columbus (arrived in the New World)
      pre-exist — live or exist before

inter- means "between."

      interstate — between the states

intra- and **intro-** are different spellings of the same prefix which means "in" or "within."

      intrastate — within a state

extra- and **extro-** are the opposite of **intra-/intro-**, and they mean "outside."

      extraterrestrial — outside the earth (Remember E.T.?)

Finally, there is another prefix that means "before:" **ante-**. This is sometimes confused with **anti-**, which means "against" (See Lesson 6). This is not a common prefix, but here are a few examples:

      antecedent — something that comes before
      anteroom — a waiting room
      ante meridian (a.m.) — before the sun reaches the meridian at noon

Exercises

A. Some bases normally take a **pre**- prefix, some normally take a **post**- prefix, and some can take either. Try to put the following bases in the right column.

caution	graduate	war	-judice
-pone	colonial	-dict	-natal (birth)
view	-pare (get ready)	trial	-vent
school	mature	pay	-scription
historic	Moslem		script (p.s.)

PRE-   *POST-*   *PRE- and/or POST-*

_____ _____ _____

_____ _____ _____

_____ _____ _____

_____ _____ _____

_____ _____ _____

_____ _____ _____

B. Use one of the words in the list below in one of the sentences. Use each word only once.

international	intersection	interview
intermediate	intermission	interpreter
interstate	interrupt	intercollegiate

1. At the concert I saw her during the _____.

2. When you apply for a job, you often go for an _____.

3. The United Nations is an _____ organization.

4. I wish you wouldn't _____ me when I am talking.

5. She works as a French - English _____.

6. She is studying German at the _____ level.

7. The store is located at the _____ of Main Street and 3rd Avenue.

8. _____ basketball is played by university and college teams.

9. The _____ highway goes through six states.

C. Read the following sentences and give a definition for the underlined word.

1. He participated in many <u>extracurricular</u> activities when he was at the university: football, debating club, political science club, and university newspaper.

   Extracurricular = _____

   _____

2. Although he didn't play intercollegiate football, he did play in the <u>intramural</u> league. I think he played for his dormitory team.

   Intramural = _____

   _____

3. The Starship Enterprise was designed for <u>extragalactic</u> travel. It often travels beyond the "Milky Way" galaxy.

   Extragalactic = _____

   _____

4. She is very friendly — a real <u>extrovert</u>. He is a shy <u>introvert</u>.

   Extrovert = _____

   _____

   Introvert = _____

   _____

5. The patient could not eat. We had to feed him <u>intravenously</u>.

   Intravenously = _____

   _____

6. It was an <u>extraordinary</u> story—front-page news.

   Extraordinary = _____

   _____

7. Meditation and yoga are forms of <u>introspection</u>.

   Introspection = _____

   _____

8. Some people believe in ESP (<u>extrasensory</u> perception) and mind reading.

   Extrasensory = _____

   _____

D. Read the following article through once for general comprehension. Then look for all the position prefixes. Then read for detailed comprehension.

Disarmament Talks Agenda Prepared

Representatives of the United Democratic Republic and the Union of Socialist States met again today in Interval for the third day of preliminary talks to set the agenda for the forthcoming disarmament conference. The preconference talks are scheduled to end tomorrow.

In a brief interview held during the morning intersession, the USS representative I.V. Tokov speaking through an interpreter, predicted that unless the UDR introduced a totally new issue, the agenda would soon be set for next Friday's conference. Asked for a preview of the agenda, Tokov said that a number of significant points were being discussed, among these a limitation on intercontinental ballistic missiles and a reduction on intermediate range missiles. A limit on the production of supersonic interceptors, however, will not appear on the agenda.

Asked if there was substance to the rumor that the conference might be postponed due to the ill health of the U.S.S. Foreign Minister, Tokov asserted that the Foreign Minister had assured him that he would allow nothing to interfere with the upcoming conference.

Tokov released a statement from the Foreign Minister, who said, "The international community is hoping for and deserves some extraordinary gains from this conference, and I will not allow illness to prevent my participation. We expect this to be the most significant disarmament conference of the postwar era. This conference is a prelude to peace," he continued, "and we are proceeding on the assumption that the goal is not just peace in our time, but rather peace for posterity. The conference is too important to be interrupted by postnasal drip."

Later in the day in a separate interview, the UDR representative A. F. Kooler indicated, however, that although the UDR is "prepared to discuss disarmament openly and positively, it is a bit premature to speculate on postconference results. We too, want peace," he said, "but the prerequisite to peace is careful and balanced negotiation at the negotiating table. Sound agreements must precede a true peace," he concluded.

***Words with position prefixes** pre-, post-, intro-, extra-:*

Lesson 16

Relationship Prefixes: super-, sur-, sub-, para-, epi-, hyper-, hypo-

The prefixes in this lesson express the idea of a relationship. They modify the base to show that the new word is either, "beyond" or "more than" the base or "beneath" or "less than" the base. For example:

> **superscript** — written above, such as 10^2
> **subscript** — written below, such as H_2O

The "super" prefixes are:

> **super** — above, over, extra, additional
> **sur** — above, over, additional
> **epi** — above, over, around, additional
> **hyper** — above, over, excessive
> **para** — beyond, outside, near, outside

The "sub" prefixes are:

> **sub** — under, beneath, less than
> **hypo** — below, beneath

With some words the **b** in **sub-** changes to the first consonant of the base, or it is dropped. For example:

succeed	**supply**
suffix	**surrender**
suggest	**suspect**

Exercises

A.   Use the prefix **super-** with one of the bases below to fill in the blanks in the sentence below.

-natural	-sonic	-fluous	-visor	-stitious
-sede	-powers	-impose	-ficial	-star

1.   That plane flies faster than sound. It is _____ .

2.   My boss is my _____ .

3.   The USSR and the USA are both _____ .

4.   Michael Jackson is a _____ .

5.   Ghosts are _____ beings.

6.   She doesn't like the number 13. She is _____ .

7.   The injuries are not deep or dangerous. They are _____ .

8.   To position one thing on top of another means to _____ one on the other.

9.   His remarks were not necessary. They were _____ .

10. These new regulations replace the old ones; they _____ the old ones.

B.   Give the meaning of the underlined words in the following sentences.

1.   She was appointed to an important <u>subcommittee</u>.

   _____

2.   The Trident missile can be launched from a <u>submerged submarine</u>.

   _____

   _____

3.   Let's take the <u>subway</u>; It's faster than the bus.

   _____

4.   The government will support the farmers with a price <u>subsidy</u>.

   _____

5.   The flood waters finally <u>subsided</u>.

   _____

6.   After the countries <u>suspended</u> peace talks, the negotiator <u>submitted</u> a new proposal.

   _____

   _____

7.   Do you <u>subscribe</u> to any magazines?

   _____

8.   These plants grow in a <u>subtropical</u> climate.

   _____

9.   They live outside the city in the <u>suburbs</u>.

   _____

10. The Central Bank should reduce the money <u>supply</u>.

   _____

11. Accept no <u>substitute</u>. Buy the real thing!

      _____

12. He was <u>suspected</u> of <u>subversive</u> activity against the government.

      _____

      _____

C. Use a **sur-** prefix with these bases in the following sentences.

-name   -passed   -charge   -prise   -face

-tax   -plus   -vivors   -vey

1. There is a 3% _____.

2. There were no _____. Everybody died.

3. What a _____! I didn't expect to see you here.

4. Please write your _____ on this line.

5. Is there a _____ for service on this bill?

6. The plane was hit by a _____-to-air missile.

7. The wheat crop has _____ our expectations. We will have a huge _____.

8. In a recent _____, the government found that 75% of all households have a TV.

D. Match the following words and phrases.

1. _____ epicenter   a. to restate something

2. _____ episode   b. an apparent contradiction

3. _____ hyperactive   c. one who says one thing, but does another

4. _____ hypothesis   d. always separated by the same distance

5. _____ hypocrite   e. an assumption

6. _____ paradox   f. like a chapter in a story

7. _____ paragraph   g. a fixed limit

8. _____ parallel   h. above the origin of an earthquake

9. _____ parameter   i. a division in writing

10. _____ paraphrase   j. overly active

E. Read the following story for general comprehension. Then find all the words with relationship prefixes.

Subcommittee Reports on Subversive Activity

The Subcommittee on un-Nordic Activity today published its annual survey of subversive activity. The subcommittee's findings came as no surprise to most observers. Among the conclusions and recommendations were:

• A plan has been submitted to the Interior Ministry to establish a permanent bureau to coordinate and supervise the surveillance of all suspected subversive activity. All government agencies now involved in the investigation of subversive activity would be subordinated to the proposed Superbureau of Investigation (SBI).

• Support for the clandestine International Anarchist Union has subsided in the state of Novgorovia. The state security office has also announced the formation of a new paramilitary unit to aid in the suppression of IAU terrorism. The unit will be equipped with automatic rifles and submachine guns.

• The mystery surrounding the September bombing of the Novgorovian hydro-electric substation has finally been dispelled. According to the subcommittee, the substation was not bombed, as originally supposed, by the IAU, but was destroyed by an angry employee who had been fired for insubordination.

• Superspy Dr. Oui, who surrendered to agent James Stock on the subtropical island of Epicuria, did not succeed in passing on significant secrets to Sudistan. However, Oui's accomplice Kitty Hawk, who is now suspected of supplying secret plans of the supersonic X-200 fighter, still has not surfaced.

SUPERSPY Dr. Oui and Kitty Hawk   INTERPOL FILE XX

• Detective supervisor Gridlock Homes, who survived an assassination attempt in a suburban subway station with only superficial wounds, has identified his assailant as a member of the Nordic underground. Apparently the attacker escaped in one of Nordurbia's many subterranean passageways.

Words with relationship prefixes super-, sur-, sub-, para-:

Lesson 17

Movement Prefixes: ex-, in-/im-, ad-, ab-, trans-, pro-

This group of prefixes usually carries a meaning of movement in some direction: "out of," "into," "away from," "across," and "in front of."

ex- means "out of" or "from." For example:

> **to export** — to carry (or send) out of a country.

In some cases the prefix is only **e-**.

> **erupt** — to break out

- *Note: there is also another* ex- *prefix which always has a hyphen and means "former" or "previous:"* ex-president — *former president*

in- is also spelled **im-** when it is attached to a word that begins with **b, m,** or **p.** It means "in," "into," or "within."

> **income** — (money) that comes in
> **import** — to carry (or bring) into a country

ad- and **ab-** have opposite meanings. **ad-** means "toward" or "to." **ab-** means "away from" or "from."

> **administer** — to serve to
> **abduct** — to lead from

The prefix **ad-** is often spelled with just the **a-**, and the first consonant of the base is doubled:

> **a + fix = affix**   **a + cept = accept**   **a + tain = attain**

trans- means "across."

> **transportation** — carrying something across (from one place to another)

pro- means "in front of" or "forward."

> **to proceed** — to move forward (**ceed** or **cede** is from Latin, and means "move.")

- *Note: there is also a* pro- *prefix that is usually hyphenated and means "for" or "in support of." For example:* pro-life — *in support of life (This phrase is often used for the position of those who are against abortion.)*

Exercises

A. Use the words in the list below and match them with a definition.

explode   expatriate   expand
income   immigrate   investigate
input   inhabitant   export
informant

1. _____ To become larger.

2. _____ To move into a new country.

3. _____ A person who lives outside his native country.

4. _____ A bomb does this.

5. _____ To study something.

6. _____ To send goods out of a country.

7. _____ Money that a person earns.

8. _____ To enter information into a computer.

9. _____ A person who lives in a place.

10. _____ A person who gives information.

B. Try to analyze and define the underlined words. If analysis doesn't help, study the context.

1. The abductors are holding a hostage.

    _____

2. He was an advisor to the president.

    _____

3. We will have to absorb the loss.

    _____

4. They continue to adhere to the policy of non-violence.

    _____

5. The weather has been abnormal.

    _____

6. The -ly suffix usually indicates an adverb.

    _____

7. In that country abortion is illegal.

    _____

8. Who will administer the test?

    _____

9. Adapting to a new culture is not always easy.

    _____

C.   Use each of the words below in one of the sentences.

transitive   transcontinental   transplant
transfer   transmitter   transportation
translate   transactions

1.   Can you _____ this into German?

2.   This radio _____ is very powerful. It can send signals thousands of kilometers.

3.   Which form of _____ will you take, bus or train?

4.   He took a _____ flight from Senegal to Somalia.

5.   This is a _____ verb; it requires an object.

6.   The surgeons performed a successful heart _____ and the patient is doing well.

7.   She made three _____ at her bank today.

8.   I want to _____ from this department to another.

D.   Match the following words with an appropriate phrase

1.   _____ proceed   a. the act of making something

2.   _____ proposal   b. to act or speak against something

3.   _____ prosecute   c. to continue

4.   _____ propeller   d. an idea to be discussed or considered

5.   _____ progress   e. to make something continue in time

6.   _____ production   f. one who supports or speaks for something

7.   _____ progressive   g. to bring action against someone in a court of law

8.   _____ protest   h. forward-looking

9.   _____ proponent   i. something that moves an airplane

10. _____ prolong   j. positive development, moving forward

E. Read the following article and then find all the words with prefixes of movement.

Exports Exceed Imports

The Ministry of Finance and Trade yesterday announced that for the first quarter of the year, the total value of exports has exceeded imports for the first time since 1986.

The shift is due mostly to a significant increase in textile and electronic exports. According to a ministry spokesperson, "our intensive, three-year expansion of the textile industry has finally paid off. In fact, our textile production is even ahead of the projections we made when we initiated the project. So far, all indications are that the prospects for the remainder of the year are excellent."

The government also claimed that the investment in the development of the electronics sector has paid off and that income from the sales of electronics equipment is also beyond all expectations.

The maritime transportation project, however, has not progressed according to plan. Admitting that the government shipbuilding yards have fallen behind schedule, the Minister of Transportation blamed part of the reduced productivity at the Porthaven Shipyard on the prolonged shipfitters' strike last fall. The Minister has promised a full-scale investigation of the slow pace of construction of transoceanic cargo carriers.

First quarter imports were only slightly ahead of last year's first quarter. The administration claimed that its intensive "Buy Domestic" campaign is a major reason for the slow growth of imported goods. "Our automotive industry is making a successful transition from the production of full-scale models to economy cars, and the consumer reaction has been positive. The Toyota invasion is over," asserted a government spokesperson.

The Ministry of Tourism also announced that the influx of tourists from Western Transfluvia has injected a considerable amount of foreign exchange into the economy.

"All in all," according to the Director of the Central Bank, "we are looking forward to a protracted period of economic progress, and although consumer prices rose somewhat in the first quarter, we are slowly winning the war against inflation and the budget deficit."

Words with prefixes of movement ex, in-, im-, ad-, ab-, trans-, pro-:

Lesson 18

Movement Prefixes: de-, re-, se-

Although these prefixes generally suggest some kind of movement, their exact meanings are not always easy to see.

de- in Latin has a meaning of "from." But as an English prefix it can also mean "down," "away from," or "the opposite of (the base)." Look at this list of words to get a general understanding of the meaning of de-:

down	*away from*	*opposite*
decrease	detain	deforestation
descend	deject	deregulate
deflate	defend	depopulate

● *Note: A hyphen may separate de- from its base when the base begins with e. For example, de-escalate.*

re- in Latin means "back" or "again." Study these words in order to get an understanding of re-:

back	*again*
retain	reforestation
reject	reissue
return	reconfirm
reclaim	rebuild

● *Note: Like de-, a hyphen may be used to separate* re- *from its base when the base begins with e. For example, re-elect.*

se- has a general meaning of "aside," "by itself," or "apart from." The meaning of **se-** is not easy to see, and it is not hyphenated.

seclude	separate
select	seduce

Exercises

A. Add either **de-** or **re-** to these bases to make a meaningful word.

1. A _____odorant is used to counteract unpleasant smells.

2. "I shall _____turn," said General MacAthur as he left the Philippines.

3. The physicist Nils Groenig _____ceived an award for his _____search.

4. The opposite of attach is _____tach.

5. It is not a genuine piece of art; it is a _____production.

6. The terrorists' objective is to _____stabilize the government.

7. We were not told the truth; we were _____ceived.

8. The government has just _____leased new information on the disastrous _____forestation of the tropical rain forests.

B. Choose the best word for the sentence.

1. As the flood waters began to (secede/recede) the people returned to their houses.

2. That man has a very high opinion of himself; in other words, his ego is (deflated/inflated).

3. The hot-air balloon crashed when it became (deflated/inflated).

4. The doctors tried everything but the patient's condition continued to (decline/recline).

5. The Lazy-Boy chair is for relaxing or lying back. It is also called a (reclining/declining) chair.

6. (Segregation/Congregation) is a form of discrimination because it means to isolate or separate one group from another.

7. The president was (selected/re-elected) for a second term of office.

8. The American Embassy in Moscow was destroyed because it was impossible to (debug/rebug) the new building. (*Bug* is a slang word meaning to install a listening device, *a bug*.)

C. Match the words below with the definition:

a. _____ cut off the head

b. _____ place authority in local hands

c. _____ cut back or cut down

d. _____ make something turn aside or away

e. _____ deteriorate or decay - lose value

f. _____ get off an airplane

g. _____ summarize, restate

h. _____ throw or bend back from a surface, like a mirror

i. _____ grow again

j. _____ bring back to life

k. _____ cause to think again or remember

1.	reflect	4.	recapitulate	7.	revive	10.	decrease
2.	decapitate	5.	decentralize	8.	deplane	11.	degenerate
3.	deflect	6.	regenerate	9.	remind		

D. Use each of the following words only once to fill in the blanks in the following sentences:

reflect	recapitulated	revive	decreased
decapitated	decentralize	deplane	degeneration
deflected	regenerate	reminded	

1. Please stay in your seats with your seat belts fastened until we reach the airport terminal and the captain gives the signal for us to _____.

2. This octopus has only seven legs because one was cut off, but since it is able to _____, it will soon grow another leg.

3. The rescue team pulled the man from the water and tried to _____ him by administering mouth-to-mouth resuscitation.

4. In the French Revolution many people, not only the king and queen, lost their heads or were _____.

5. The statement you have just heard does not _____ the view of the management

6. In his speech he _____ the nation that the road to progress was difficult.

7. The village was saved because a rocky hill just above it _____ the landslide.

8. _____ or loss of muscle control is a feature of Parkinson's disease.

9. The chairman of the committee _____ the points discussed and then called for a vote.

10. France realized that it was necessary to _____ its banking procedures, as it was too time consuming for all transactions to flow through the central bank in Paris.

11. A decompression chamber is used for divers whose bodies need to have pressure _____ slowly.

E.   Read the following article for general comprehension. Then search for the de-, re- and se- prefixes.

Students Demand Chancellor's Resignation

Students at the National University in Estlania gathered outside the administration building Friday afternoon and chanted "Retire or rehire," directing their demands at the university chancellor. The chancellor recently dismissed half of the English faculty in the foreign language department on the grounds that the expatriate English instructors were from degenerate societies and consequently their potentially destructive influence could destabilize Estlanian society.

The chancellor declared that English would continue to be taught, but that the instructors would be replaced by local staff. The courses are to be restructured with emphasis on the grammar and a substantial reduction in cultural content.

The decisions are part of the government's efforts to detach itself from the West. Recognizing that it cannot totally divorce itself from the West, however, the government announced that only fields related to national finance and security would remain untouched. A special group of students will be selected to continue studies in language and subjects related to business, finance and defense. These students will be employed by the government for whatever projects require contact or advanced knowledge or technology from the West.

The protesting students from the group Students for Free Expression, want the

UNIVERSITY CHANCELLOR   MJP

chancellor deposed, instructors reinstated, and the library restocked with the books and other materials that have been removed. The student association has talked of bringing suit against the government for withholding information and reducing the quality of Estlanian education. When asked about the charges, a government spokesman declined to comment.

For the past two days the chancellor has remained in seclusion in his living quarters, and has been unavailable for comment.

Words with* de-, re- *and* se- *prefixes:

Lesson 19

"With" and "Against" Prefixes: syn-, co-, contra-

The prefixes in this lesson modify the meaning of the base by adding a meaning of either "togetherness" or "opposition to" the base meaning.

syn- is also spelled **sym-** before **b**, **m**, or **p**. It means "sharing with" or "together."

    sympathy — feeling with or for (someone)

co-, which generally means "together," "with," or "equally," has several variant spellings: **con-**, **col-**, **com-**, and **cor-**. It is joined to a long list of Latin bases, and in many cases the "together" meaning is not easy to see. Therefore, analysis is not always helpful for understanding co- words.

    cooperate — work together
    collapse — fall together
    conduct — lead together/with
    compress — push together
    correspond — answer back (and forth) together

contra- and a closely related form **counter-** have a meaning of "against" or "opposite."

    contradict — say the opposite
    counteract — act against

There is also a prefix **ob-**, with variant spellings **op-**, **oc-**, **of-** and **o-**, which can have a meaning of "against" or "facing," as in **opposite**, "to be positioned against."

Exercises

A.   In column 2 are some "syn" words. Can you use them to fill in the blanks in column 1 to create a common phrase?

	1	2
1.	a _____ shape	symbol
2.	_____ and analysis	sympathetic
3.	a _____ person	symphony
4.	a _____ orchestra	symmetrical
5.	_____ and antonym	symptoms
6.	a religious _____	synchronized
7.	_____ of a disease	synonym
8.	_____ movements	synthesis

B.   In these sentences try to explain the meaning of contra- and counter- words. If analysis of the word does not help you, study the context.

1.   Turn the dial in a counterclockwise direction.
     Counterclockwise _____
     _____

2.   Contraception techniques are taught in birth-control clinics.
     Contraception _____
     _____

3.   There are many counterfeit $ 100 bills in circulation.
     Counterfeit _____
     _____

4.   We need to agree on this, so please don't contradict me.
     Contradict _____
     _____

5.   This traveler's check has not been countersigned.
     Countersigned _____
     _____

6.   In some places birth control is a very controversial subject.
     Controversial _____
     _____

7.   After the initial battle, the defenders counterattacked.
     Counterattack _____
     _____

8.   The negotiator refused to continue the dialogue with his counterpart.
     Counterpart _____
     _____

9.   The identity of our counterspy cannot be revealed. It must remain secret.
     Counterspy _____
     _____

10. Some people called the hippy movement of the 60's a countercultural revolution.
     Countercultural _____
     _____

C.   com- is prefixed to bases that begin with b, m, or p. Can you guess what con-, col-, and cor- are prefixed to? Add a prefix to these bases.

_____ bine	_____ pare	_____ struct
_____ cept	_____ pose	_____ relation
_____ rect	_____ serve	_____ fident
_____ lect	_____ lateral	_____ lide
_____ form	_____ mercial	_____ trol
_____ vict	_____ nect	_____ junction

D. con- is a common prefix. Here are some sentences from previous readings. Can you explain the con words? These words are not always easy to analyze, so study the **context**.

1. The detainees were under investigation for criminal <u>conspiracy</u>.

   _____

   _____

2. The list of arrests may grow as the investigation <u>continues</u>.

   _____

   _____

3. A spokesman has <u>confirmed</u> that the airliner was carrying tourists.

   _____

   _____

4. They will begin a search for the wreckage when weather <u>conditions</u> permit.

   _____

   _____

5. The novel was acclaimed as a major <u>contribution</u> to world literature.

   _____

   _____

6. He is the resident <u>conductor</u> at the Thyme <u>conservatory</u> of music.

   _____

   _____

7. Robert Rackham is a well-known forestry <u>consultant</u>.

   _____

   _____

8. He claimed the <u>Conservative</u> Union Party was apathetic.

   _____

   _____

9. He <u>concluded</u> by saying that his party would be victorious again.

   _____

   _____

10. He covered up his <u>conviction</u> in 1981 for embezzling funds from the First Andean Bank.

    _____

    _____

11. <u>Condolences</u> poured into the capital of Territoria as the citizens began a three-day mourning for the death of R. J. Lee. _____

12. Plastic explosives are made of very flexible material that is easily <u>concealable</u>.

    _____

    _____

13. Mainland coastal areas <u>contain</u> nearly one-third of the world's population.

    _____

    _____

14. They met to set the agenda for the forthcoming disarmament conference.

    _____

    _____

15. The minister promised an investigation of the slow pace of construction of transoceanic cargo carriers.

    _____

    _____

16. Consumer prices rose somewhat in the first quarter.

    _____

    _____

E. Read the following passage for general comprehension. Then go through it again looking for all the words with syn-, con-, and contra- prefixes.

Union Sympathizers Walk off the Job

Yesterday morning over 350 Transcontinental Airways pilots and flight attendants refused to cross picket lines of the striking Ground Crew Union, leaving thousands of passengers stranded. Airports throughout the eastern part of the country were congested with angry commuters and travellers. Incoming passengers at Concordia Airport were forced to seek ground connections to the many regional cities serviced by TCA.

Meanwhile, union negotiators, meeting with TCA officials, rejected a compromise solution to the widening conflict between management and employees. TCA had offered a 10% salary increase in response to the union's demands for a 15% pay hike. The collapse of the talks came after seven consecutive days of collective bargaining. At the heart of the contract dispute is the union's insistence that their salaries have not kept pace with inflation. "Our salaries have remained constant for two years now, while inflation continues to constrict the purchasing power of our income," complained one angry baggage handler.

At a press conference late yesterday afternoon, an airline spokesman said, "We want to cooperate with the union. Coexistence is our goal, but according to our consultants, our offer to the union matches what our competitors are paying. We made a sincere offer to the negotiators, hoping to avoid this confrontation, but our counterparts have simply chosen to be contrary."

Contacted at his Contracoastal beach condominium, Meriwether P. Barnstormer, principal owner of TCA issued a brief comment on the crisis: "I am confident we will find a satisfactory conclusion to this confusion. TCA however, will not be coerced into signing a contract that would compel us to increase air fares, and I am convinced that the union's demands would force us to do just that."

Asked if the pilots' walkout was simply a one-day gesture, striking pilot Harlan Wing insisted that the pilots were 100% behind the Ground Crew Union. According to Wing, the conflict is actually a symptom of some very serious differences between Barnstormer and the airline he controls.

Words with syn-, con-, *and* contra- *prefixes:*

Lesson 20

Some Common Bases

Most of the work in this book has focused on affixes, which are attached to bases. Sometimes the base is a word, like **fix**. Sometimes the base is not a word itself, like **plod**, as in **explode**.

Many bases that are not words by themselves come from Latin. The list of Latin bases that are used in English is very long, and it is not possible to memorize the list. It would be like trying to memorize a small dictionary. However, there are some Latin bases that occur frequently in English. In this lesson we will look at some of the most common bases.

Exercises.

A1. The bases in this exercise all suggest some kind of **motion**. Match the motion word below with the underlined bases in the sentences.

Motion Words:

a. carry

b. move

c. send

d. go in steps

e. move along

f. lead

Sentences:

1. _____ He con<u>duct</u>ed the Thyme Orchestra.

2. _____ <u>Gra</u>dually the fighting subsided.

3. _____ Let's pro<u>ceed</u> carefully. This is an important decision.

4. _____ Let's bring a <u>port</u>able radio with us.

5. _____ He didn't lose his job, but he was de<u>mot</u>ed, and his salary

    was reduced.

6. _____ This radio can trans<u>mit</u> a signal for 100 kilometers.

A2. Now give a simple definition of these words:

deduct _____

graduate _____

intercede _____

export _____

promote _____

remit _____

B1.   The bases in this exercise all have a general meaning of **action**. match these action words with the underlined base in the sentences.

Action Words:

a. get, take   d. throw   f. hold, keep
b. happen   e. break   g. pull
c. close, shut

Sentences:

1. _____ The instructions were not in<u>clud</u>ed in the package.

2. _____ He never re<u>ceiv</u>ed my proposal.

3. _____ The astronauts' safety capsule was e<u>ject</u>ed from their spacecraft.

4. _____ The dentist ex<u>tract</u>ed all his wisdom teeth.

5. _____ The de<u>tain</u>ee tried to escape

6. _____ The strike has di<u>srupt</u>ed air travel throughout the East.

7. _____ We met by coin<u>cid</u>ence; it wasn't planned.

B.2   Now give a simple definition of these words.

conclude _____

recipient _____

reject _____

subtract _____

retain _____

erupt _____

incident _____

C1. These bases have a variety of meanings. Match the words below with the underlined base in the sentences.

Words:

a. talk, shout   d. rule, manage   f. middle
b. write   e. believe, trust   g. stretch, tighten
c. say

Sentences:

1. _____ The bank is going to give him <u>cred</u>it.

2. _____ After three days of in<u>tens</u>ive talks, the negotiations collapsed.

3. _____ "No!" he ex<u>claim</u>ed.

4. _____ The di<u>rect</u>or will see you in his office.

5. _____ Some people think they can pre<u>dict</u> the future.

6. _____ They are reducing the number of inter<u>med</u>iate range missiles.

7. _____ Can you pre<u>scrib</u>e some medicine for me?

C2. Now give a simple definition of these words.

discredit _____

tension _____

claimant _____

regulate _____

dictator _____

mediate _____

inscription _____

D. In the following reading, look for the bases that have been studied in this lesson. Then look at the reading and locate all the affixes you have studied. Do not locate the inflectional affixes of Lesson 1. List your findings on page 72.

"Incredible Mission" Accomplished

World Celebrates Final Vote

Today at the United Nations Headquarters in New York, the 162 members of the United Nations General Assembly unanimously passed a resolution to support the Superpower Disarmament Treaty (SDT), thereby concluding months of gradual progress toward peace. The peace talks, conceived in Oslo over two years ago, have been described as "Earth's Incredible Mission." Today's resolution, coinciding with the anniversary of the nuclear destruction of Hiroshima, brought the "incredible mission" to a dramatic and successful conclusion.

ONE PEACEFUL WORLD

The SDT, which was signed two weeks ago in Geneva, has been proclaimed by world leaders and ordinary citizens everywhere as the crowning achievement of the 20th century. In a century that has included the horrors of two world wars, regional conflicts on virtually every continent, and countless local and civil wars, as well as a prolonged cold war between the West and East Bloc nations, the SDT at last offers the possibility of global peace in the 21st century.

The superpowers, after months of prolonged talks, announced two weeks ago, a complicated plan for the orderly destruction of all nuclear weaponry, a significant reduction of conventional forces, and a surveillance plan to be conducted by the United Nations Peacekeeping Force. The UN force will be staffed only with non-superpower military contingents.

The crucial second phase of the SDT Treaty, which dictated that all non-nuclear nations also submit their military establishments to observation by UN intermediaries, was considered by many detractors to be the potential stumbling block to the total plan. In support of the second phase, peace groups around the world have staged numerous demonstrations and waged an intensive media campaign directed at the General Assembly. After two weeks of intense debate, as the eyes of the world watched, the General Assembly voted. As Zaire, Zambia and Zimbabwe cast the final affirmative votes, the entire Assembly rose to its feet in applause.

Outside the UN Headquarters, a crowd estimated at over 100,000 people, watching the proceedings on mobile TV monitors, waved thousands of blue flags bearing the symbolic peace dove.

As the news was transmitted around the world, spontaneous celebrations erupted in thousands of cities and towns.

Congratulatory messages from leaders of the Peace Movement and thousands of private citizens poured into the national capitals of the superpowers and U.N. Headquarters.

The Secretary General, in a press conference shortly after the final vote, praised the efforts of the peacemakers. He also injected a cautionary note, reminding the people of the world that the hard task of maintaining peace had only begun.

Bases: Affixes:

ANSWERS

LESSON 1

● *Note: Words repeated in the news articles are given only once in the answer key.*

Uncovered ● detained ● suspected ● terrorists ● discovered ● explosives ● hidden ● weapons ● taken ● raided ● locations ● prevented ● prosecutor's ● detainees ● according ● sources ● planning ● carried ● unnamed ● neighboring ● officers ● warrants ● issued ● ringleaders ● agents ● investigations ● handling ● agency's ● largest ● expected ● arrests ● longer ● continues ● Feds

LESSON 2

Exercise A

1. One who speaks for another
2. A leader, especially of an illegal group
3. Secret
4. To collect, gather or bring together
5. A place where goods are stored

Exercise B

1. Failure of the heart
2. A conservative political group
3. Seven people who belong to a group
4. A stop to war
5. A period of five years
6. At an important position
7. Supported by the government
8. Exempt from import tax
9. A trip to a place and back
   Having no smoke
10. Two identical engines

Exercise E

Airliner ● Aircraft ● outbound ● turbojet ● state-owned ● airline NATIONAIR ● fighter-bomber ● takeoff ● Gulfside ● Airport ● hour-long ● eyewitnesses ● midair ● twin-engine ● jetliner ● thunderstorm ● daybreak ● spokeswoman ● planeload ● seaside ● Air-sea ● rainstorm ● shark-infested ● lifejackets ● air-miles ● mainland ● frogmen ● underwater

LESSON 3

Exercise A

reporter	planner	marcher	demonstrator
creditor	commander	kidnapper	advisor, adviser
writer	inspector	director	supporter
professor	exporter	designer	governor
buyer	farmer	trader	murderer
leader	hijacker	voter	forecaster
manager	liar	rioter	actor
employer	traveler, traveller	lawyer	interpreter
prosecutor	investigator	foreigner	officer
worker	laborer	survivor	defector
flyer, flier	negotiator	dealer	
prisoner		photographer	

Exercise B

1. passenger
2. doctor
3. member
4. soldier
5. ambassador
6. mayor
7. traitor
8. chancellor
9. minister
10. neighbor
11. victor

Exercise C

1. i   2. c   3. g   4. h   5. d   6. a
7. k   8. f   9. j   10. e   11. b

Exercise D

1. employee — employer
2. detainee
3. trainer — trainee
4. payer , payor — payee
5. addressee
6. profiteer
7. pamphleteer
8. racketeer
9. auctioneer
10. volunteer
11. engineer

Exercise E

Negotiator ● Kidnappers ● Ambassador ● reporters ● captors ● members ● prisoners ● adviser ● interpreter - leader ● foreigners ● workers ● travelers ● mayor ● councilors ● demonsrators ● marchers ● supporters ● commander ● detainees ● investigator

LESSON 4

Exercise A

1. scientist
2. sociologists, psychologists, psychiatrists
3. economist, capitalists, socialists, communists
4. dramatist, novelist, columnist
5. guitarist, violinist, pianist, cellist, flutist
6. realists, idealists
7. activist, anarchist, environmentalist, ecologist
8. arsonist, terrorist, rapist
9. tourist, motorist

Exercise B

1. b   2. e   3. a   4. f   5. c   6. d

Exercise C

1. migrant
2. opponent
3. consultant
4. accountant
5. occupant
6. patient
7. immigrant
8. dissident
9. resident

Exercise D

1. armory
2. bakery
3. dictionary
4. directory
5 diary
6. laboratory
7. library
8. treasury
9. factory
10. territory
11. mortuary
12. chemistry

Exercise F

One who

Artists ● Scientists ● winners ● panelist ● physicist ● assistants ● Professor ● botanist ● chemist ● novelist ● dramatist ● Antillian ● recipient ● Idealist ● author ● dissident ● resident ● composer ● pianist ● musicians ● proponent ● conductor ● environmentalist ● consultant ● activist ● proletarian ● Capitalist

Place where

laboratory ● diary ● Conservatory ● forestry

LESSON 5

Exercise B

independent	imperfect	imbalance	insane
immature	immoral	insecure	illiterate
irresponsible	incapable	illogical	improper
indefinite	indirect	irrational	

Exercise C

1. nonsmoker
2. non-Moslem
3. nonaligned
4. nonstop
5. nonviolence
6. nonsense
7. nontoxic
8. nonconformist
9. nonpayment
10. non-Arab
11. nonmember
12. nonperforming

Exercise D

Nonresident • Independent • illegally • uninterested • illegal • unattractive • unrewarding • unemployment • unskilled • uneducated • illiterate • irresponsible • unlimited • non-Lowlanders • inadequate • unrest • unemployed

• *Note: anti-Highlander is also a negative word. We will study* anti- *in the next lesson.*

LESSON 6

Exercise A

1. antiaircraft: used against aircraft
2. antiabortion: opposing or against abortion
3. antipathy: opposite feeling
4. Anti-semitism: against semites (or Jews)
5. antitrust: regulation against trusts
6. antonyms: opposite word or meaning

Exercise B

atypical	amoral	anonymous	apathy
anarchy	anesthetic	amorphous	anaerobic
apolitical	asexual	atheism	asymmetry

Exercise D

misbehave	malnutrition	mismanage	misplace	mislead
misjudge	misprint	malfunction	malpractice	maladjusted
misfortune	malcontent	misguide	misfit	misspell

Exercise E

Disagree • differentiated • diverse • apathetic • antipollution • mismanagement • unregulated • anarchy • malcontents • misfits • disruption • disturbance • Anti-Everything Party • misguided • maladjusted • atheists • misappropriated • malignant • misled • misinformed • dismissed • malpractice • malnutrition • divisive • amoral • opposition • unworthy • misgovernment • mistake • misplaced • misfired

LESSON 7

Exercise A

1. two
2. three
3. unicycle
4. having one language
5. having two languages
6. the same distance
7. trilingual
8. having many languages
9. all
10. monochromatic
11. tri
12. many
13. bilateral
14. uni
15. half of a colon
16. every 6 months or half the year
17. semiprivate
18. semicircle
19. multinational
20. equilateral

Exercise B

multimedia	semicircular	multimillionaire	semiprecious
bimonthly, semimonthly	bifocal	multipurpose	bicentenary
multiskilled, semiskilled	semifinal	multicultural, bicultural	equidistant
multivitamin			

Exercise C

Polyglot: speaking many languages   multilingual: speaking many languages
bilingual: speaking two languages   monotony: one tone (boring)
bimonthly: twice a month or every two months

Exercise D

Pan-Equatorian • semi-annual • multibillion • tri-state • equidistant • monorail • unify • multitude • multilingual • trilingual • bilingual • Polytechnic • biennial • bilateral

LESSON 8

Exercise A

soften	widen	entrust	endorse
endanger	enclose	loosen	encourage
enable	engage	endure	encounter
deepen	brighten	enforce	enhance
employ	weaken	embrace	engulf

Exercise B

| 1. betrayed | 3. bereaved, bemoaned | 5. behooves | 7. belittle | 9. beclouded |
| 2. bewildering | 4. bedevilled | 6. Beware | 8. besieged | |

Exercise C

1. demonstrate	4. dramatized	7. negotiated	10. terrorized
2. immigrate	5. assassinated	8. graduate	11. legalized
3. nationalize	6. investigate	9. operate	12. speculate

Exercise D

identify	activate	capitalize
classify	locate	equalize
falsify	tolerate	civilize
unify	appropriate	idealize
simplify	differentiate	romanticize
intensify		finalize
certify		

Exercise E

Intensifies • prosecution • strengthen • testify • operating • distributes • identified • terrorized • located • characterizing • centralize • distributors • immigrated • naturalized • falsified • naturalization • embezzling • employed • speculating • bewildered • besieged • investigated • enforcement • recognize • classified • betray • assassinate • frighten • prosecute

LESSON 9

Exercise A

intelligence	agency	assistance	difference
assurance	disappearance	dissidence	conference
presidency	residence	democracy	independence
conspiracy	residency	insistence	
disturbance		preference	
candidacy		illiteracy	

Exercise B

1. similarity	3. familiarity	5. equality	7. activity
2. humanity	4. captivity	6. simplicity	8. Security

Exercise C

1. steadiness	4. stillness	7. carelessness	9. foolishness
2. unworthiness	5. kindness	8. helpfulness	10. busyness, carefulness, business
3. correctness	6. hopelessness		

Exercise D

1. citizenship	4. leadership	7. craftsmanship	9. Brotherhood
2. statehood	5. childhood	8. dictatorship	10. statesmanship
3. neighborhood	6. censorship		

Exercise E

Independence • condolences • residence • neighborhood • Brotherhood • ownership • apprenticeship • experiences • Unity • disobedience • prominence • democracy • candidacy • Equality • Opportunity • nationhood • fairness • tolerance • minority • dictatorship • presidency • statesmanship • adherence • non-violence • Conference

LESSON 10

Exercise A

investigate	demonstrate	pollute	provide
locate	acclaim	disrupt	graduate
prevent	contribute	reject	cooperate
prosecute	immigrate	indicate	recognize
collide	oppose	conclude	elect
confirm	errupt	organize	operate
identify	administer	present	explode

Exercise B

appointment	management	criticise (x)	contribute (x)	movement
announcement	government	development	compose (x)	
expect (x)	statement	requirement	establishment	

Exercise C

conservatism (a conservative)
criticism (a critic)

Exercise D

1. wreckage	5. sewage, sewerage	9. carriage	13. marriage
2. coverage	6. postage	10. spoilage	14. baggage
3. footage	7. freedom	11. martyrdom	15. breakage
4. stardom	8. package	12. boredom	16. brokerage

Exercise E

Assassination • Investigation • government • declaration • administration • Kingdom • terrorism • identification • announcement • Information • Freedom • faction • Organization • Nationalism • martyrdom • Department's • direction • television • footage • speculation • carriage • reception • explosion • package • wreckage • statement • disruption • continuation

LESSON 11

Exercise A

believable	possible	responsible	considerable
permissible	acceptable	tolerable	credible
receivable	measurable	reasonable	manageable
questionable	operable	predictable	defendable
advisable		defensible	

Exercise B

1. recognizable
2. tolerable
3. odorless
   colorless
   detectable
4. likeable
5. enjoyable
6. collapsible
7. fruitless
8. flexible
9. hopeless
10. fashionable

Exercise C

1. wooden
2. suicidal
3. oral
4. optional
5. floral
6. oval
7. woolen, thermal
8. golden
9. formal
10. earthen

Exercise D

1. e   2. i   3. g   4. a   5. c   6. h   7. d   8. j   9. b   10. f

Exercise E

Undetectable ● Illegal ● detectable ● odorless ● material ● helpless ● flexible ● concealable ● impossible defenseless ● recognizable ● powerless ● identifiable ● profitable -controversial

LESSON 12

Exercise A

migratory birds: birds that move from one place to another
respiratory illness: a problem with breathing
purposeful activity: an activity with a purpose
dangerous weapon: a weapon that can be harmful
scandalous affair: a shameful matter
monotonous sound: a sound that does not change (boring)
helpful advise: useful information
skillful politician: a clever politician
snowy weather: a snowstorm
silky fabric: cloth that is like silk
starry sky: a sky full of stars

Exercise B

1. hopeful	4. culinary	7. infectious	10. luxurious
2. cautious	5. careful	8. greasy, starchy	
3. revolutionary	6. precautionary	9. foggy	

Exercise C

ridiculous	greedy	fictitious	icy	purposeful
oily	ambitious	stringy	melodious	visionary
thankful	thoughtful	faithful	pearly	
scary	inflationary	envious	secondary	

Exercise D

snowy	chilly	icy	sunny	cloudy
windy	foggy	hazy	rainy	misty
muddy	dusty	smoky	smoggy	

Exercise E

Disastrous • mountainous • rocky • temporary • voluntary • -primary • powerful • unwary • ordinary • Regulatory • sturdy • hilly • dangerous • previous • rainy • sandy • secondary • generous • thoughtful • parliamentary • military

LESSON 13

Exercise A

1. heroic	4. brownish	7. creative
2. schizophrenic	5. boyish, comic	8. foolish
3. constructive destructive	6. selfish	9. acidic

Exercise B

1. metallic	4. conclusive	7. organic	10. collective
2. sluggish	5. girlish, fortyish	8. fantastic	
3. microscopic	6. geometric	9. brackish	

Exercise C

1. greenish	4. ticklish	7. metric
2. grayish	5. scientific	8. corrective
3. attractive	6. italic	9. basic

Exercise D

NOUN	VERB
magnet	magnetize
telephone	telephone
system	systematize
explosion	explode
creation, creativity	create
defense	defend
conclusion	conclude
disruption	disrupt
progression, progress	progress
decision	decide
production	produce

Exercise E

Turkish	Swedish	English	Danish	Scottish
Finnish	Irish	Spanish	British	

Exercise F

Dramatic ● idyllic ● massive ● extensive ● frantic ● heroic ● sluggish ● destructive ● feverish ● classic ● unselfish ● decisive ● terrific

LESSON 14

Exercise A

federally	ideally	responsibly	cleverly
automatically	environmentally	nationally	independently
apparently	conservatively	appropriately	democratically
intelligently	illegally	immediately	fairly
normally	financially	peacefully	progressively
politically	steadily	successfully	securely

Exercise B

1. steadily
2. actively
3. fairly
4. securely
5. successfully
6. conservatively
7. normally
8. nationally
9. Apparently
10. environmentally
11. immediately
12. peacefully
13. illegally
14. automatically
15. appropriately

Exercise C

1. d   2. g   3. h   4. a   5. j   6. i   7. e   8. b   9. f   10. c

Exercise D

1. downward	4. lengthwise	7. Budgetwise	10. inward
2. skyward	5. backward	8. toward	
3. outward	6. homeward	9. forward	

Exercise E

Urgently ● internationally ● dramatically ● invariably ● steadily ● globally ● directly ● indirectly ● significantly ● Accordingly ● principally ● sorely ● certainly ● potentially ● politically ● economically ● densely ● especially ● partially ● completely ● severely ● nearly ● Additionally ● drastically ● increasingly ● currently ● immediately ● forward ● backward

LESSON 15

Exercise A

Pre		*Post*	*Pre and/or Post*	
precaution	premature	postpone	prewar	postwar
preview	pre-Moslem	postgraduate	pre-trial	post-trial
preschool	predict	postscript	prepay	postpay
prehistoric	prejudice		prenatal	postnatal
prepare	prevent			
	prescription			

Exercise B

1. intermission	4. interrupt	7. intersection
2. interview	5. interpreter	8. Intercollegiate
3. international	6. intermediate	9. interstate

Exercise C

1. extracurricular: not part of the regular curriculum
2. intramural: internal; within the walls of the university
3. extragalactic: beyond our galaxy
4. extrovert: outgoing; interested in others
   introvert: inward-looking; interested in one's own thoughts
5. intravenously: within the veins
6. extraordinary: beyond the ordinary; unusual
7. introspection: self-examination
8. extrasensory: outside normal senses

Exercise D

Prepared ● Interval ● preliminary ● preconference ● interview ● intersession ● interpreter ● predicted ● introduced ● preview ● intercontinental ● intermediate ● interceptors ● postponed ● interfere ● international ● extraordinary ● prevent ● postwar ● prelude ● posterity ● interrupted ● postnasal ● premature ● postconference ● prerequisite ● precede

LESSON 16

Exercise A

1. supersonic
2. supervisor
3. superpowers
4. superstar
5. supernatural
6. superstitious
7. superficial
8. superimpose
9. superfluous
10. supersede

Exercise B

1. subcommittee: division of a larger committee
2. submerged: went under water
   submarine: ship that operates under water
3. subway: a way under-ground; metro
4. subsidy: price support
5. subsided: went back (receded)
6. suspended: stopped
   submitted: handed in
7. subscribe: receive regularly
8. subtropical: zone between the tropical and temperate regions
9. suburbs: outside the city
10. supply: source
11. substitute: a replacement for something
12. suspected: thought to be
    subversive: working against

Exercise C

1. surtax
2. survivors
3. surprise
4. surname
5. surcharge
6. surface
7. surpassed
   surplus
8. survey

Exercise D

1. h   2. f   3. j   4. e   5. c   6. b   7. i   8. d   9. g   10. a

Exercise E

Subcommittee ● Subversive ● survey ● surprise ● submitted ● supervise ● surveillance ● suspected ● subordinated ● Superbureau ● support ● subsided ● paramilitary ● suppression ● submachine ● surrounding ● substation ● supposed ● insubordination ● Superspy ● surrendered ● subtropical ● succeed ● supplying ● supersonic ● surfaced ● supervisor ● survived ● suburban ● subway ● superficial ● subterranean

LESSON 17

Exercise A

1. expand
2. immigrate
3. expatriate
4. explode
5. investigate
6. export
7. income
8. input
9. inhabitant
10. informant

Exercise B

1. abductors: those who carry away; kidnappers
2. advisor: one who sees something; gives advice to
3. absorb: take up; accept
4. adhere: stick to
5. abnormal: away from or not normal
6. adverb: modifies a verb (or adjective)
7. abortion: taking something away; especially an unborn baby
8. administer: conduct; give
9. adapting: fitting into; adjusting to

Exercise C

1. translate
2. transmitter
3. transportation
4. transcontinental
5. transitive
6. transplant
7. transactions
8. transfer

Exercise D

1. c   2. d   3. g   4. i   5. j   6. a   7. h   8. b   9. f   10. e

Exercise E

Export ● Exceed ● Imports ● increase ● intensive ● expansion ● industry ● production ● projections ● initiated ● project ● indications ● prospects ● excellent ● investment ● income ● expectations ● transportation ● progressed ● productivity ● prolonged ● promised ● investigation ● transoceanic ● imported ● transition ● invasion ● asserted ● influx ● Transfluvia ● injected ● exchange ● protracted ● progress ● inflation

LESSON 18

Exercise A

1. de
2. re
3. re, re
4. de
5. re
6. de
7. de
8. re, de

Exercise B

1. recede
2. inflated
3. deflated
4. decline
5. reclining
6. Segregation
7. re-elected
8. debug

Exercise C

a. 2
b. 5
c. 10
d. 3
e. 11
f. 8
g. 4
h. 1
i. 6
j. 7
k. 9

Exercise D

1. deplane
2. regenerate
3. revive
4. decapitated
5. reflect
6. reminded
7. deflected
8. Degeneration
9. recapitulated
10. decentralize
11. decreased

Exercise E

Demand • Resignation • Retire • rehire • department • degenerate • destructive • destabilize • declared • replaced • restructured • reduction • decisions • detach • recognizing • related • remain • selected • defense • require • Expression • deposed • reinstated • restocked • removed • reducing • declined • remained • seclusion

LESSON 19

Exercise A

1. a symmetrical shape
2. a synthesis and analysis
3. a sympathetic person
4. a symphony orchestra
5. synonym and antonym
6. a religious symbol
7. symptoms of a disease
8. synchronized movements

Exercise B

1. counterclockwise: against the normal progression of the clock, i.e., backwards
2. contraception: to prevent conception
or the fertilization of an egg
3. counterfeit: illegally printed
4. contradict: say the opposite
5. countersigned: a second, confirming signature
6. controversial: an issue having opposite points of view
7. counterattack: to return an attack
8. counterpart: someone who has a similar position
9. counterspy: a spy who tries to catch spies
10. countercultural: against the traditional culture

Exercise C

combine	compare	construct
concept	compose	correlation
correct	conserve	confident
collect	collateral	collide
conform	commercial	control
convict	connect	conjunction

Exercise D

1. conspiracy: to breathe together, i.e., an illegal plan or group
2. continues: to remain in existence
3. confirmed: to state as true
4. condition: a state of being
5. contribution: something that is given
6. conductor: leader of a group (of musicians)
   conservatory: a school of music
7. consultant: one who is consulted; one who supplies advice
8. conservative: a point of view that preserves the usual order; moderate, cautious
9. concluded: to bring to an end
10. conviction: to be found guilty
11. condolences: expressions of sorrow
12. concealable: can be hidden
13. contain: to enclose or include
14. conference: a meeting to discuss something
15. construction: the act of building
16. consumer: one who uses, like a customer

Exercise E

Sympathizers • congested • commuters • Concordia • connection • compromise • conflict • collapse • consecutive • collective • contract • constant • continues • constrict • complained • conference • cooperate • Coexistence • consultants • competitors • confrontation • counterparts • contrary • Contacted • Contracoastal • condominium • comment • confident • conclusion • confusion • coerced • compel • convinced • conflict • symptom • controls

LESSON 20

Exercise A1

1. f	2. d	3. e	4. a	5. b	6.c

Exercise A2

deduct: to lead from (subtract)
graduate: to go in a series of steps (leave school)
intercede: to move between (mediate)

export: to carry out (trade)
promote: to move forward (in a career)
remit: to send (back) especially money

Exercise B1

1. c	2. a	3. d	4. g	5. f	6. e	7. b

Exercise B2

conclude: to bring to a close
recipient: one who receives
reject: to throw back (or away)
subtract: to pull down (reduce)

retain: to hold (back)
erupt: to break out (explode)
incident: happening

Exercise C1

1. e	2. g	3. a	4. d	5. c	6. f	7. b

Exercise C2

discredit: to take away trust
tension: tightness
claimant: one who asks for something
regulate: to direct or control

dictator: one who says what to do
mediate: to come between
inscription: something written in or on something

Exercise D

Bases

Incredible • mission • support • concluding
gradual • progress • conceived • described
coinciding • successful • conclusion • proclaimed
included • continent • reduction • conducted
contingents • dictated • submit • intermediaries
detractors • intensive • media • directed
proceedings • mobile • transmitted • erupted
injected • maintaining

Exercise D

Affixes

Incr**edible**
accomplished
Nat**ions**
memb**ers**
Gener**al**
unanim**ously**
resolut**ion**
support
superpower
Disarma**ment**
concluding
grad**ual**
progress
to**ward**
conceived
described
coinciding
destruct**ion**
dramat**ic**
success**ful**
conclus**ion**
proclaimed
ordin**ary**
achieve**ment**
included
region**al**
conflicts
continent
count**less**
prolonged
poss**ibility**
glob**al**
compli**cated**
order**ly**
destruct**ion**
weapon**ry**
signific**ant**
reduct**ion**
convention**al**
surveill**ance**

conducted
non-superpower
milit**ary**
conting**ents**
cruci**al**
dict**ated**
non-nuclear
submit
establish**ments**
observ**ation**
intermediaries
considered
detract**ors**
potenti**al**
support
numer**ous**
demonstrations
intens**ive**
debate
affirm**ative**
fin**al**
applause
estim**ated**
proceedings
monit**ors**
sym**bolic**
transmitted
spontane**ous**
erupted
congratul**atory**
lead**ers**
move**ment**
nation**al**
secret**ary**
confer**ence**
short**ly**
peacemak**ers**
injected
caut**ionary**
reminding

Glossary of Bases

Base	*Meaning*	*Examples*
arch	rule, lead	anarchy, monarch, monarchy
cap	chief, head	capital, decapitate
capt, cept, cep, cip, ceive	get, take	captor, captive, accept, intercept, reception, recipient, receive, conceive
cede, ceed, cess	go, move	precede, intercede, proceed, exceed succeed, process
ceive(see capt)		
cep(t)(see capt)		
cide, cis	happen	decide, coincide, decision
claim, clam	talk, shout	acclamation, acclaim
clud, clus	close, shut	include, conclude, seclusion
cord	agree	accord; discord
creas	grow	increase, decrease
cred	believe, trust in	credence, incredible, creditor
cur	run	currently, occur
dict	say	predict, dictate, indicate, dictionary
duce, duct	lead	produce, reduce, introduce, production, conduct, abduct
dol	sorrow	condolence
fact, fect	make, do	factory, faction, defector, perfect
fer	carry, bear	transfer, interfere, conference
fin	end, complete	final, indefinite
firm	make solid	affirmative, confirm
flat	blow	inflate, deflate, inflation
flect, flex	bend	reflect, deflect, flexible
fug	run, move	refugee, refuge
fus	pour	confuse, diffuse, refuse
grad, gress	go, step	gradual, graduate, progress
ject	throw	project, reject, inject, subject
jud, jur	judge	judicial, jury
lect	choose	select, elect, collect
leg	law	illegal, legislature
lide, lis	strike, move	collide, collision
lit	read	illiterate, literacy
logy	study	ecology, psychology
med	middle	intermediary, immediately, media
migra	move	migratory, immigration
minis	help, serve	minister, administration
miss, mit	send	mission, commission, dismiss, permit, transmit, submit
mob, mot	move	mobile, automotive
nat	birth, nature	nation, nature, naturalize
nym	name	anonymous, antonym, synonym
ord	order	ordinary, orderly, insubordination
pathy	feeling	sympathy, antipathy, apathy
pel	push	compel, dispel, expel
pend	hang, wait	independent, suspend
plaud, plod	clap, noise	applaud, explode

Base	Meaning	Examples
plex, plic	fold	complex, complicate
plod (see plaud)		
port	carry	export, import, support, report, transportation
pon, pos	place, put	proponent, postpone, composer, propose, depose, exposure
press	push down	suppress, express
quest	look for, ask	question, request
rect, regul	rule, manage	director, regulatory, unregulated
rupt	break	erupt, disrupt, interrupt, corruption
secut, sequ	follow	consecutive, prosecutor, consequently
scrib, scrip	write	scripture, describe
serv	save	conservative, preserve, observation
side	live, sit	resident, president, subside
sist(see stat)		
spec, spect	see, watch, look at	suspect, inspect, expect, prospect, speculate
spir	breathe	conspiracy, respiratory
spon	answer, promise	response, irresponsible
stat, sist, stit	stand	status, state, assistant, insist, institute
struct	build	constructive, destruction, restructure, instruct
sum	take (up)	assume, resume, consume
tain, tin	hold, keep	contain, attain, detain, continue
tens	stretch, tighten	intensive, extensive
terr	earth	territory, terrestrial, terrain
tort	twist, bend	torture, distort
tract	pull	tractor, contract, detractor, attractive, protracted
var	change	variety, variant, invariably
vent	come	venture, prevent, conventional
vers, vert	turn, change	diverse, subversive, divert
vestig	follow, track	investigate, investigation
vic, vinc	win, defeat	convict, convince, victorious
vid, vis	see	provide, advise, vision, supervise,
viv	live	survivor, revive
voc, vok	call	vocal, revoke, invoke
volv	turn	involve, revolve